Here is a Quiz Book which provides a lot of fun and information all at the same time. You can solve the clues with your friends or by yourself. This book can be used in two ways. Either by yourself, when you answer the questions like a crossword puzzle and write your answers in the spaces provided, or it can be used as a game with one or more friends. One can be the quizmaster and two others the competitors, each competitor trying to get a linking pattern of hexagons, one across and the other down.

Marshall Pickering
An imprint of HarperCollins*Publishers*
77—85 Fulham Palace Road
Hammersmith, London W6 8JB

First published in 1989 by Marshall Morgan and Scott
Publications Ltd

9 8 7 6 5 4 3 2

A catalogue record for this book
is available from the British Library

Printed in Great Britain by
HarperCollinsManufacturing, Glasgow

Bible Blockbusters

Based on the New International Version of the Bible

Suitable for Bible classes, youth clubs and adult Bible study groups.

Cyril Barnes

CENTRAL

Based on the Central Independent Television series produced in association with Mark Goodson Productions and Talbot Television Ltd.

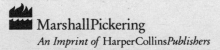

MarshallPickering
An Imprint of HarperCollinsPublishers

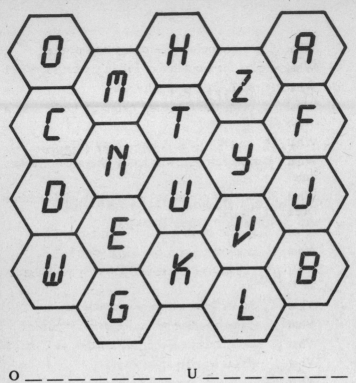

O _ _ _ _ _ _ _ _   U _ _ _ _ _ _

C _ _ _ _ _ _ _ _   K _ _ _ _ _ _

D _ _ _ _ _ _ _ _   Z _ _ _ _ _ _

W _ _ _ _ _ _ _ _   Y _ _ _ _ _ _

M _ _ _ _ _ _ _ _   V _ _ _ _ _ _

N _ _ _ _ _ _ _ _   L _ _ _ _ _ _

E _ _ _ _ _ _ _ _   A _ _ _ _ _ _

G _ _ _ _ _ _ _ _   F _ _ _ _ _ _

H _ _ _ _ _ _ _ _   J _ _ _ _ _ _

T _ _ _ _ _ _ _ _   B _ _ _ _ _ _

O: What 'O' comes before heard, lay and power?

C: What 'C' was the mountain of Elijah's great sacrifice?

D: What 'D' is an extremely salty sea?

W: What 'W' with the Christian name of Leslie was a Methodist preacher?

M: What 'M' of Bible days is now called Iraq?

N: What 'N' was a Jezreelite who had a vineyard in David's time?

E: What 'E' was an orphaned Jewish girl who became Queen of Persia?

G: What 'G' should be said before eating a meal?

H: What 'H' is another term for the godless?

T: What 'T' were opened by the Magi as they worshipped the baby Jesus?

U: What 'U' comes before take, stand and go?

K: What 'K' is the meaning of an Egyptian Pharaoh?

Z: What 'Z' was the name given to Barnabas in Lystra?

Y: What 'Y' means to give up or over?

V: What 'V' is another term for triumph and rests with the Lord?

L: What 'L' in the Psalms is a legendary monster?

A: What 'A' visited a house in Straight Street, Damascus, to help to convert Saul?

F: What 'F' comes before ever, given and saken?

J: What 'J' was the home of Bede, the English historian?

B: What 'B' ring in a church tower and decorate a priest's robe?

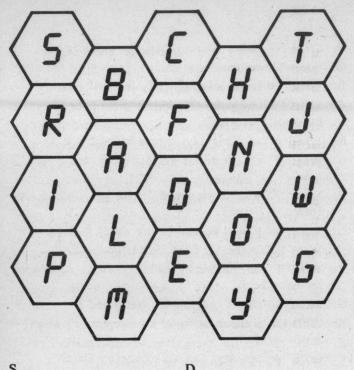

S _ _ _ _ _ _ _ _ D _ _ _ _ _ _ _

R _ _ _ _ _ _ _ _ E _ _ _ _ _ _

I _ _ _ _ _ _ _   H _ _ _ _ _ _ _

P _ _ _ _ _ _ _   N _ _ _ _ _ _

B _ _ _ _ _ _   O _ _ _ _ _ _ _

A _ _ _ _ _ _ _   Y _ _ _ _ _ _ _

L _ _ _ _ _ _ _   T _ _ _ _ _ _ _

M _ _ _ _ _ _ _   J _ _ _ _ _ _ _

C _ _ _ _ _ _ _   W _ _ _ _ _ _ _

F _ _ _ _ _ _ _   G _ _ _ _ _ _ _

S: What 'S' was the main legislative body in New Testament Jerusalem?

R: What 'R' was a shepherd-girl who married Jacob?

I: What 'I' is wrongly worshipped by some people?

P: What 'P' was the Roman governor who judged Jesus?

B: What 'B' is a tower connected with the confusion of languages?

A: What 'A' was, according to the Bible, the first man?

L: What 'L' were special priests in Old Testament worship?

M: What 'M' was found by an Egyptian princess as he floated in a papyrus basket?

C: What 'C' was Queen of Ethiopia whose treasurer was an early Christian convert?

F: What 'F' were used to make a poultice to cure Hezekiah's boil?

D: What 'D' was a prisoner-of-war who became provincial ruler of Babylon?

E: What 'E' was the boy Samuel's leader in Shiloh?

H: What 'H' is another word for blessed?

N: What 'N' was where Paul wanted to see Titus during the winter?

O: What 'O' comes before look, run and flow?

Y: What 'Y' must we not do to temptation but encourage the land to do?

T: What 'T' was the trade of Simon of Joppa?

J: What 'J' was banished to the island of Patmos?

W: What 'W' was a Charles and hymnwriter?

G: What 'G' was a proconsul of Achaia when Paul was brought into court in Corinth?

B _ _ _ _ _ _ _ _ _	N _ _ _ _ _ _ _
D _ _ _ _ _ _ _ _ _	J _ _ _ _ _ _ _
O _ _ _ _ _ _ _ _ _	F _ _ _ _ _ _ _
R _ _ _ _ _ _ _ _ _	S _ _ _ _ _ _ _
T _ _ _ _ _ _ _ _	M _ _ _ _ _ _ _
L _ _ _ _ _ _ _ _	G _ _ _ _ _ _ _
A _ _ _ _ _ _ _ _	P _ _ _ _ _ _ _
K _ _ _ _ _ _ _ _	Q _ _ _ _ _ _ _
H _ _ _ _ _ _ _ _	C _ _ _ _ _ _ _
E _ _ _ _ _ _ _ _	I _ _ _ _ _ _ _

B: What 'B' is the head of a Church of England diocese?

D: What 'D' is another name for Satan?

O: What 'O' was the scene of the martyrdom of Cranmer, Latimer and Ridley?

R: What 'R' was a dry camp where Moses struck a rock and water poured out?

T: What 'T' was the Caesar when John the Baptist began his ministry?

L: What 'L' was a doctor and gospel writer?

A: What 'A' is the title of the head of the Church of England?

K: What 'K' was a Scottish religious reformer who once took refuge in the Castle of St Andrews?

H: What 'H' comes before Bible, Ghost and Land?

E: What 'E' was the home of the Pharaohs?

N: What 'N' was a Syrian healed from leprosy in the River Jordan?

J: What 'J' was once a Jebusite city and became the home of Judah's kings?

F: What 'F' did Jesus use to write on the ground?

S: What 'S' is a musical term appearing in many psalms?

M: What 'M' is the island where Paul was shipwrecked?

G: What 'G' comes before post, way and keeper?

P: What 'P' was where Paul met a Jewish sorcerer named Bar-Jesus?

Q: What 'Q' was blown in from the sea as an evening meal for the wandering Israelites?

C: What 'C' was a faithful explorer into the Valley of Eshcol?

I: What 'I' was a sixteenth-century soldier who gave up his sword and founded the Jesuits?

F _ _ _ _ _ _ _ _   P _ _ _ _ _ _ _ _

K _ _ _ _ _ _ _ _   T _ _ _ _ _ _ _ _

U _ _ _ _ _ _ _ _   S _ _ _ _ _ _ _ _

V _ _ _ _ _ _ _ _   B _ _ _ _ _ _ _ _

A _ _ _ _ _ _ _ _   N _ _ _ _ _ _ _ _

E _ _ _ _ _ _ _ _   M _ _ _ _ _ _ _ _

C _ _ _ _ _ _ _ _   H _ _ _ _ _ _ _ _

R _ _ _ _ _ _ _ _   O _ _ _ _ _ _ _ _

I _ _ _ _ _ _ _ _   D _ _ _ _ _ _ _ _

G _ _ _ _ _ _ _ _   L _ _ _ _ _ _ _ _

F: What 'F' was a governor in Caesarea who also had the name of Porcius?

K: What 'K' was a black civil rights leader who was awarded the Nobel Peace Prize in 1964?

U: What 'U' was the relationship of Laban to Jacob?

V: What 'V' is a city within a city in Italy?

A: What 'A' was the town of Joseph who offered his tomb for the burial of Jesus?

E: What 'E' was a left-handed Benjamite who made an eighteen-inch double-edged sword?

C: What 'C' was Peter's Aramaic name?

R: What 'R' is a cathedral near the Medway?

I: What 'I' was Eli's son-in-law with a name that meant 'no glory'?

G: What 'G' is a worldwide evangelist from America who was born in 1918?

P: What 'P' met another traveller on the Gaza road?

T: What 'T' were collected by Matthew?

S: What 'S' helped to bring spices to anoint the body of Jesus?

B: What 'B' comes before any, el and ul?

N: What 'N' was a town which Nathaniel thought could produce nothing good?

M: What 'M' is the name of a gospel and a square in Venice?

H: What 'H' was a hymnwriter with the Christian names of William Walsham?

O: What 'O' stages a famous passion play every ten years?

D: What 'D' is a Greek letter and a river mouth like the Nile?

L: What 'L' was a Scottish missionary who took medicine and Christianity to Central Africa in 1840?

H _ _ _ _ _ _ _ _   L _ _ _ _ _ _ _
F _ _ _ _ _ _ _ _   W _ _ _ _ _ _ _
O _ _ _ _ _ _ _ _   G _ _ _ _ _ _ _
N _ _ _ _ _ _ _ _   C _ _ _ _ _ _ _
S _ _ _ _ _ _ _ _   J _ _ _ _ _ _ _
D _ _ _ _ _ _ _ _   R _ _ _ _ _ _ _
P _ _ _ _ _ _ _ _   U _ _ _ _ _ _ _
E _ _ _ _ _ _ _ _   I _ _ _ _ _ _ _
M _ _ _ _ _ _ _ _   A _ _ _ _ _ _ _
B _ _ _ _ _ _ _ _   T _ _ _ _ _ _ _

H: What 'H' was a king of Aram anointed by Elijah?

F: What 'F' has a king who is a Methodist?

O: What 'O' provided Solomon with four tons of gold?

N: What 'N' built an ark and survived a great flood?

S: What 'S' was anointed king while looking for his father's lost donkeys?

D: What 'D' loved the world too much and forsook Paul?

P: What 'P' had a slave named Onesimus who was converted while a runaway?

E: What 'E' was the biblical name for Abyssinia?

M: What 'M' is an Old Testament book meaning messenger?

B: What 'B' was a Philistine garrison in David's day and also had the name of Ephrath?

L: What 'L' is the palace home of the Archbishop of Canterbury?

W: What 'W' is a Bible colour describing snow, hair and light?

G: What 'G' taught Paul his theology in Jerusalem?

C: What 'C' was an Irishman who took Christianity to the highlands of Scotland?

J: What 'J' is the river the Israelites crossed to reach the promised land?

R: What 'R' is the book of the Bible sometimes called the Apocalypse?

U: What 'U' was a Hittite whose widow married King David?

I: What 'I' did Paul travel through to reach Rome?

A: What 'A' was a prophet who was also a shepherd in Tekoa?

T: What 'T' is a Cornish cathedral, the first to be erected in Britain after the building of St Paul's?

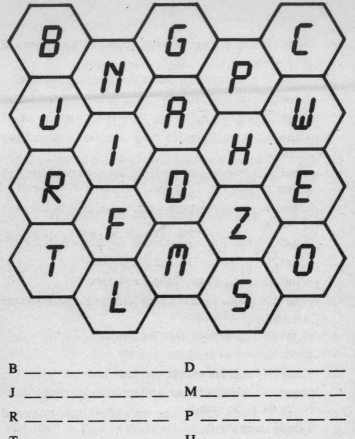

B _ _ _ _ _ _ _ _

J _ _ _ _ _ _ _ _

R _ _ _ _ _ _ _ _

T _ _ _ _ _ _ _ _

N _ _ _ _ _ _ _ _

I _ _ _ _ _ _ _ _

F _ _ _ _ _ _ _ _

L _ _ _ _ _ _ _ _

G _ _ _ _ _ _ _ _

A _ _ _ _ _ _ _ _

D _ _ _ _ _ _ _ _

M _ _ _ _ _ _ _ _

P _ _ _ _ _ _ _ _

H _ _ _ _ _ _ _ _

Z _ _ _ _ _ _ _ _

S _ _ _ _ _ _ _ _

C _ _ _ _ _ _ _ _

W _ _ _ _ _ _ _ _

E _ _ _ _ _ _ _ _

O _ _ _ _ _ _ _ _

B: What 'B' was a Cypriot who helped Paul on some of his travels?

J: What 'J' is sometimes called the weeping prophet?

R: What 'R' was a Moabite woman, an ancestor of Jesus?

T: What 'T' was the day when Jesus rose from the dead?

N: What 'N' is an Egyptian river that flows from Lake Victoria?

I: What 'I' is an island in the Hebrides with an abbey and graves of kings of Scotland, Ireland and Norway?

F: What 'F' was the second plague in Egypt in the days of Moses?

L: What 'L' was the instigator of the Reformation?

G: What 'G' precedes Orthodox Church?

A: What 'A' were Peter, James and John?

D: What 'D' was the Italian poet born in 1265 who wrote 'La Divina Commedia'?

M: What 'M' is another title for Christ?

P: What 'P' are early Bibles written on?

H: What 'H' was the mother of Samuel?

Z: What 'Z' was the father of James and John?

S: What 'S' was a strong man who killed three thousand people as he died?

C: What 'C' was the place of Mary Slessor's missionary work?

W: What 'W' is the London area where The Salvation Army began?

E: What 'E' went up to heaven in a chariot of fire?

O: What 'O' hid and fed a hundred prophets during a famine in Ahab's reign?

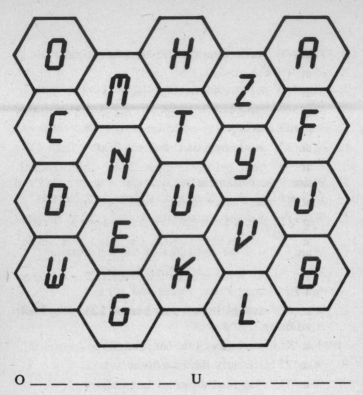

O _ _ _ _ _ _ _ _   U _ _ _ _ _ _

C _ _ _ _ _ _ _ _   K _ _ _ _ _ _

D _ _ _ _ _ _ _ _   Z _ _ _ _ _ _

W _ _ _ _ _ _ _ _   Y _ _ _ _ _ _

M _ _ _ _ _ _ _ _   V _ _ _ _ _ _

N _ _ _ _ _ _ _ _   L _ _ _ _ _ _

E _ _ _ _ _ _ _ _   A _ _ _ _ _ _

G _ _ _ _ _ _ _ _   F _ _ _ _ _ _

H _ _ _ _ _ _ _ _   J _ _ _ _ _ _

T _ _ _ _ _ _ _ _   B _ _ _ _ _ _

O: What 'O' had an iron bed thirteen feet long?

C: What 'C' was a brother of Abel?

D: What 'D' was Israel's second king?

W: What 'W' fell down in Jericho at the sound of forty-nine trumpets?

M: What 'M' was known as the Great Sea?

N: What 'N' goes before English Bible, International Version and Testament?

E: What 'E' goes before lasting, ready and green?

G: What 'G', also known as Tiberias, is a sea in Israel?

H: What 'H' is the place where the good will spend eternity?

T: What 'T' was a young man who received two letters from Paul?

U: What 'U' was the king who died when Isaiah received his vision?

K: What 'K' was a valley of rubbish and fire in Jerusalem?

Z: What 'Z' could well describe Noah's ark?

Y: What 'Y' is England's second archbishopric?

V: What 'V' was the Latin version of the Bible?

L: What 'L' goes with faith and hope?

A: What 'A' brought his brother Peter to Jesus?

F: What 'F' protected Jonah after his shipwreck?

J: What 'J' was the Christian name of Bunyan?

B: What 'B' founded The Salvation Army in 1865?

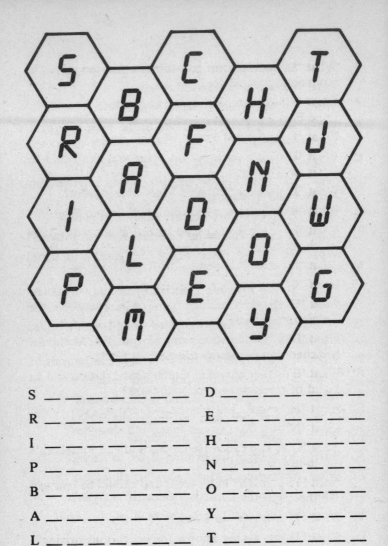

S _ _ _ _ _ _ _   D _ _ _ _ _ _ _

R _ _ _ _ _ _ _   E _ _ _ _ _ _ _

I _ _ _ _ _ _ _   H _ _ _ _ _ _ _

P _ _ _ _ _ _ _   N _ _ _ _ _ _ _

B _ _ _ _ _ _ _   O _ _ _ _ _ _ _

A _ _ _ _ _ _ _   Y _ _ _ _ _ _ _

L _ _ _ _ _ _ _   T _ _ _ _ _ _ _

M _ _ _ _ _ _ _   J _ _ _ _ _ _ _

C _ _ _ _ _ _ _   W _ _ _ _ _ _ _

F _ _ _ _ _ _ _   G _ _ _ _ _ _ _

S: What 'S' was a doctor four times over who served as a missionary in Africa?

R: What 'R' was Archbishop of Canterbury who visited Pope Pius VI in 1966?

I: What 'I' was called Persia in Bible days?

P: What 'P' was a robe put on Jesus and cloth sold by Lydia of Thyatira?

B: What 'B' was the home of Mary and Martha?

A: What 'A' is a day a week and a half before Whitsun?

L: What 'L' is a red-sandstone cathedral started in 1904 which took nearly eighty years to build?

M: What 'M' was the homeland of Ruth?

C: What 'C' was the first murderer?

F: What 'F' was the Christian name of Mendelssohn, the German composer?

D: What 'D' is the Christian name of a pacifist, Methodist preacher who became a life peer in 1965?

E: What 'E' is the festival of Christ's resurrection and an island of mysterious rock sculptures?

H: What 'H' wrote 'Tell me the old, old story'?

N: What 'N' is a doorway in many old churches?

O: What 'O' is also called Heliopolis and had Potiphera's son-in-law as priest?

Y: What 'Y' is usually in his teens and should be renewed like the eagle's?

T: What 'T' is a river in Rome?

J: What 'J' was a king known for his furious driving?

W: What 'W' is a city with both abbey and cathedral?

G: What 'G' is a river in India sacred to the Hindus?

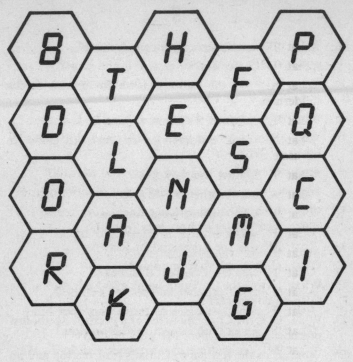

B _ _ _ _ _ _ _ _ _ _   N _ _ _ _ _ _ _ _

D _ _ _ _ _ _ _ _ _   J _ _ _ _ _ _ _ _

O _ _ _ _ _ _ _ _ _   F _ _ _ _ _ _ _ _

R _ _ _ _ _ _ _ _ _   S _ _ _ _ _ _ _ _

T _ _ _ _ _ _ _ _ _   M _ _ _ _ _ _ _ _

L _ _ _ _ _ _ _ _ _   G _ _ _ _ _ _ _ _

A _ _ _ _ _ _ _ _ _   P _ _ _ _ _ _ _ _

K _ _ _ _ _ _ _ _ _   Q _ _ _ _ _ _ _ _

H _ _ _ _ _ _ _ _ _   C _ _ _ _ _ _ _ _

E _ _ _ _ _ _ _ _ _   I _ _ _ _ _ _ _ _

B: What 'B' was Joseph's younger brother?

D: What 'D' comes before cast, fall and pour?

O: What 'O' was the daily measure for manna in the wilderness?

R: What 'R' followed Solomon as king in Jerusalem?

T: What 'T' took Solomon seven years to build in Jerusalem?

L: What 'L' follows the darkness?

A: What 'A' was brother to Moses?

K: What 'K' is an ancient word for cows?

H: What 'H' was a brother of Shem and Japheth?

E: What 'E' was the first garden?

N: What 'N' was the father of Joshua?

J: What 'J' was a prophet and son of Pethuel?

F: What 'F' does Jesus give to those who obey him?

S: What 'S' was a king known for his wisdom?

M: What 'M' was an American preacher with Ira Sankey?

G: What 'G' defeated the Midianites with three hundred men?

P: What 'P' are the songs written by David?

Q: What 'Q' was governor of Syria when Jesus was born?

C: What 'C' was a town where Jesus attended a wedding?

I: What 'I' was the Christian name of hymnwriter Watts?

F ___ ___ ___ ___ ___ ___ ___   P ___ ___ ___ ___ ___ ___ ___

K ___ ___ ___ ___ ___ ___ ___   T ___ ___ ___ ___ ___ ___ ___

U ___ ___ ___ ___ ___ ___ ___   S ___ ___ ___ ___ ___ ___ ___

V ___ ___ ___ ___ ___ ___ ___   B ___ ___ ___ ___ ___ ___ ___

A ___ ___ ___ ___ ___ ___ ___   N ___ ___ ___ ___ ___ ___ ___

E ___ ___ ___ ___ ___ ___ ___   M ___ ___ ___ ___ ___ ___ ___

C ___ ___ ___ ___ ___ ___ ___   H ___ ___ ___ ___ ___ ___ ___

R ___ ___ ___ ___ ___ ___ ___   O ___ ___ ___ ___ ___ ___ ___

I ___ ___ ___ ___ ___ ___ ___   D ___ ___ ___ ___ ___ ___ ___

G ___ ___ ___ ___ ___ ___ ___   L ___ ___ ___ ___ ___ ___ ___

F: What 'F' goes with hope and love?

K: What 'K' goes with ask and seek?

U: What 'U' comes before stairs, right and roar?

V: What 'V' is the present capital of Malta?

A: What 'A' was a group Paul met in Athens?

E: What 'E' comes before jah, sha and ab?

C: What 'C' was once one of the names of the United Reformed Church?

R: What 'R' from Adam was used to make Eve?

I: What 'I' means 'to be made flesh' and is used in connection with the birth of Jesus?

G: What 'G' was the mountain on which Jotham told a parable about trees?

P: What 'P' was the wife of Aquila?

T: What 'T' follows Elijah the?

S: What 'S' was a cricketer who became a bishop?

B: What 'B' was asking who saw writing on the wall during a banquet?

N: What 'N' was a Bible city and brother of Abraham?

M: What 'M' is another name for the three wise men?

H: What 'H' did the Psalmist pray to be cleansed with?

O: What 'O' was where Gideon threshed wheat in a winepress?

D: What 'D' was a silversmith in Ephesus?

L: What 'L' comes before prayer, supper and day?

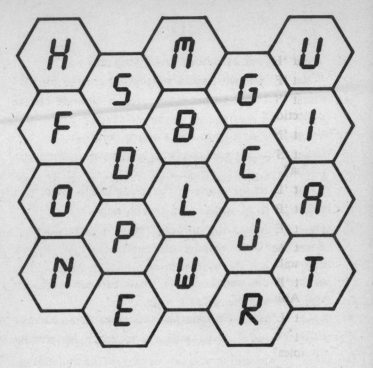

H _ _ _ _ _ _ _ _   L _ _ _ _ _ _ _
F _ _ _ _ _ _ _ _   W _ _ _ _ _ _ _
O _ _ _ _ _ _ _ _   G _ _ _ _ _ _ _
N _ _ _ _ _ _ _ _   C _ _ _ _ _ _ _
S _ _ _ _ _ _ _ _   J _ _ _ _ _ _ _
D _ _ _ _ _ _ _ _   R _ _ _ _ _ _ _
P _ _ _ _ _ _ _ _   U _ _ _ _ _ _ _
E _ _ _ _ _ _ _ _   I _ _ _ _ _ _ _
M _ _ _ _ _ _ _ _   A _ _ _ _ _ _ _
B _ _ _ _ _ _ _ _   T _ _ _ _ _ _ _

H: What 'H' comes before band, long and way?

F: What 'F' was the day in which God created birds?

O: What 'O' is another name for a church service collection?

N: What 'N' has an eye and a sharp point?

S: What 'S' was a cricketer who became a missionary in China?

D: What 'D' is the name of the ten towns in Israel?

P: What 'P' is an authorised church minister?

E: What 'E' was a Zuphite and father of Samuel?

M: What 'M' is the title of the head of the Free Church Council?

B: What 'B' was the scene of a treaty between Abraham and Abimelech?

L: What 'L' is the Christian attitude towards an enemy?

W: What 'W' did Jesus walk on to reach his rowing disciples?

G: What 'G' was a gift from the wise men to Jesus?

C: What 'C' in Rome is where many Christians were martyred?

J: What 'J' wrote three New Testament epistles?

R: What 'R' was the son of Simon who carried the cross for Jesus?

U: What 'U' were animals considered unfit to eat?

I: What 'I' means 'God with us'?

A: What 'A' was a mountain where Noah's ark came to rest?

T: What 'T' cannot be tamed and means language?

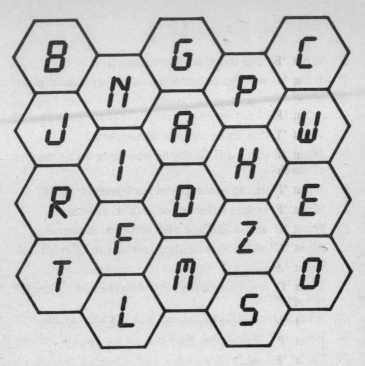

B _ _ _ _ _ _ _   D _ _ _ _ _ _ _
J _ _ _ _ _ _ _   M _ _ _ _ _ _ _
R _ _ _ _ _ _ _   P _ _ _ _ _ _ _
T _ _ _ _ _ _ _   H _ _ _ _ _ _ _
N _ _ _ _ _ _ _   Z _ _ _ _ _ _ _
I _ _ _ _ _ _ _   S _ _ _ _ _ _ _
F _ _ _ _ _ _ _   C _ _ _ _ _ _ _
L _ _ _ _ _ _ _   W _ _ _ _ _ _ _
G _ _ _ _ _ _ _   E _ _ _ _ _ _ _
A _ _ _ _ _ _ _   O _ _ _ _ _ _ _

B: What 'B' was the prince of demons?

J: What 'J' was the father of all who play the harp and flute?

R: What 'R' was the great grandmother of King David?

T: What 'T' did Luke write to in the Acts?

N: What 'N' was an Elkoshite who prophesied against Nineveh?

I: What 'I' was the second name of Judas?

F: What 'F' comes before born, fruits and rate?

L: What 'L' did Jesus bring back to life in Bethany?

G: What 'G' do Jews call people not of their race?

A: What 'A' was the father of the Apostle James?

D: What 'D' was a shepherd boy before becoming king of Israel?

M: What 'M' was the longest-living man on record?

P: What 'P' were prayer bands worn by Jews?

H: What 'H' were Jews who had adopted the Greek language?

Z: What 'Z' was the wife of Moses?

S: What 'S' did Jesus calm on the lake?

C: What 'C' was head of the temple guard?

W: What 'W' is another word for desert?

E: What 'E' is a bird known for its swift flight?

O: What 'O' is the mount of ascension?

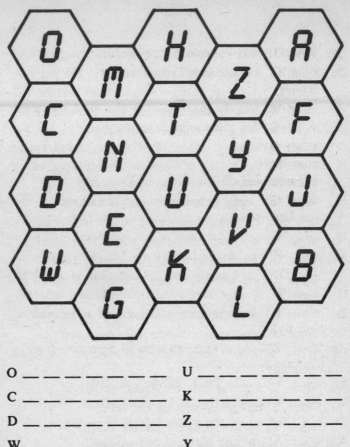

O _ _ _ _ _ _ _ _

C _ _ _ _ _ _ _ _

D _ _ _ _ _ _ _ _

W _ _ _ _ _ _ _ _

M _ _ _ _ _ _ _ _

N _ _ _ _ _ _ _ _

E _ _ _ _ _ _ _ _

G _ _ _ _ _ _ _ _

H _ _ _ _ _ _ _ _

T _ _ _ _ _ _ _ _

U _ _ _ _ _ _ _

K _ _ _ _ _ _ _

Z _ _ _ _ _ _ _

Y _ _ _ _ _ _ _

V _ _ _ _ _ _ _

L _ _ _ _ _ _ _

A _ _ _ _ _ _ _

F _ _ _ _ _ _ _

J _ _ _ _ _ _ _

B _ _ _ _ _ _ _

O: What 'O' must we do to the commandments to enter life?

C: What 'C' is also called Golgotha?

D: What 'D' was a prophetess who held court near Bethel?

W: What 'W' in a parable sprouted with the wheat?

M: What 'M' were merchants who bought Joseph for twenty shekels?

N: What 'N' was a king of Babylon who dreamed of an enormous statue?

E: What 'E' was a prophet who appeared at the transfiguration?

G: What 'G' is the colour of a hill far away?

H: What 'H' was king in Jerusalem when Jesus was born?

T: What 'T' is the name of each main division of the Bible?

U: What 'U' is associated with borrowing and interest?

K: What 'K' comes before of Kings, of Israel and of Norway?

Z: What 'Z' was a king who called Jeremiah from a dungeon to the palace?

Y: What 'Y' is easy for a follower of Jesus?

V: What 'V' is in charge of a local Anglican church?

L: What 'L' was a den where Darius threw Daniel?

A: What 'A' was the husband of Sapphira?

F: What 'F' did Jesus come to do with the law?

J: What 'J' was father-in-law to Moses?

B: What 'B' of the King of Egypt's household was put into prison with Joseph?

S _ _ _ _ _ _ _ _ —   D _ _ _ _ _ _ _
R _ _ _ _ _ _ _ _ —   E _ _ _ _ _ _ _
I _ _ _ _ _ _ _ —   H _ _ _ _ _ _ _
P _ _ _ _ _ _ _ _ —   N _ _ _ _ _ _ _
B _ _ _ _ _ _ _ _ —   O _ _ _ _ _ _ _
A _ _ _ _ _ _ _ _ —   Y _ _ _ _ _ _ _
L _ _ _ _ _ _ _ _ —   T _ _ _ _ _ _ _
M _ _ _ _ _ _ _ _ —   J _ _ _ _ _ _ _
C _ _ _ _ _ _ _ _ —   W _ _ _ _ _ _ _
F _ _ _ _ _ _ _ _ —   G _ _ _ _ _ _ _

14

S: What 'S' was the town where Jesus met a woman at a well?

R: What 'R' must never be used on the head of a Nazarite?

I: What 'I' had no room for the baby Jesus?

P: What 'P' comes before Wales, of Peace and of demons?

B: What 'B' founded homes for unwanted children?

A: What 'A' is the part of the Bible missing in some versions?

L: What 'L' is an animal and is the answer to Samson's riddle?

M: What 'M' did Barnabas sail with to Cyprus?

C: What 'C' was the home of Jesus when he heard of John the Baptist's imprisonment?

F: What 'F' comes before of Tabernacles and of Weeks?

D: What 'D' troubled Nebuchadnezzar that he could not sleep?

E: What 'E' was mother of John the Baptist?

H: What 'H' is the Bible word for pretender?

N: What 'N' was Pharaoh standing by in his first dream?

O: What 'O' was a convert of Paul's while in prison?

Y: What 'Y' were two oxen held together?

T: What 'T' is where Paul stayed for seven days on his third journey?

J: What 'J' was a Gileadite whose rash vow brought about the death of his daughter?

W: What 'W' is an abbey associated with King Harold?

G: What 'G' is a fruit a bad tree cannot bear?

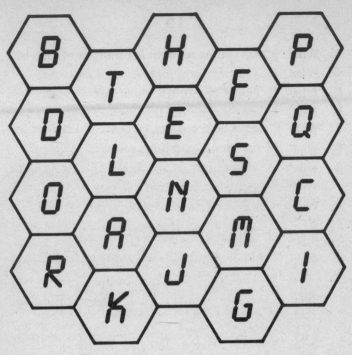

B _ _ _ _ _ _ _ _   N _ _ _ _ _ _ _ _

D _ _ _ _ _ _ _ _   J _ _ _ _ _ _ _ _

O _ _ _ _ _ _ _ _   F _ _ _ _ _ _ _ _

R _ _ _ _ _ _ _ _   S _ _ _ _ _ _ _ _

T _ _ _ _ _ _ _ _   M _ _ _ _ _ _ _ _

L _ _ _ _ _ _ _ _   G _ _ _ _ _ _ _ _

A _ _ _ _ _ _ _ _   P _ _ _ _ _ _ _ _

K _ _ _ _ _ _ _ _   Q _ _ _ _ _ _ _ _

H _ _ _ _ _ _ _ _   C _ _ _ _ _ _ _ _

E _ _ _ _ _ _ _ _   I _ _ _ _ _ _ _ _

B: What 'B' did Moses see burning on Mount Horeb?

D: What 'D' is a fruit or a number on a calendar?

O: What 'O' comes before set, shoot and spring?

R: What 'R' did Samson tell his thirty companions?

T: What 'T' did Jonah run away to?

L: What 'L' was Rebekah's brother?

A: What 'A' was a missionary who led a party of children over the mountains in China?

K: What 'K' was the father of King Saul?

H: What 'H' housed foxes although Jesus had nowhere to sleep?

E: What 'E' was the director of public works in Rome?

N: What 'N' is the road that leads to life?

J: What 'J' was a desert where John the Baptist called for repentance?

F: What 'F' is the type of man who builds his house on sand?

S: What 'S' is a cathedral with an extremely high spire?

M: What 'M' was the first son of Joseph?

G: What 'G' was nine feet tall and was killed with a stone?

P: What 'P' did Amos see the Lord holding by a wall?

Q: What 'Q' produced the stone for Solomon's temple?

C: What 'C' with a paralysed servant came to Jesus in Capernaum?

I: What 'I' was the regiment Cornelius belonged to?

F _ _ _ _ _ _ _   P _ _ _ _ _ _ _
K _ _ _ _ _ _ _   T _ _ _ _ _ _ _
U _ _ _ _ _ _ _   S _ _ _ _ _ _ _
V _ _ _ _ _ _ _   B _ _ _ _ _ _ _
A _ _ _ _ _ _ _   N _ _ _ _ _ _ _
E _ _ _ _ _ _ _   M _ _ _ _ _ _ _
C _ _ _ _ _ _ _   H _ _ _ _ _ _ _
R _ _ _ _ _ _ _   O _ _ _ _ _ _ _
I _ _ _ _ _ _ _   D _ _ _ _ _ _ _
G _ _ _ _ _ _ _   L _ _ _ _ _ _ _

F: What 'F' comes before brands, light and wood?

K: What 'K' was the tribe of the father-in-law of Moses?

U: What 'U' was King Manasseh's palace garden?

V: What 'V' did Isaiah say will be raised up or exalted?

A: What 'A' was commander of Saul's army?

E: What 'E' was thought to be Paul's nationality in the Jerusalem barracks?

C: What 'C' was an extra item found in Benjamin's sack of grain?

R: What 'R' are Christians to do when persecuted or insulted falsely?

I: What 'I' did the Psalmist ask to be forgiven and blotted out?

G: What 'G' is the title held by the head of The Salvation Army?

P: What 'P' of great value is like the kingdom of heaven?

T: What 'T' was an Ephesian seen with Paul in Jerusalem?

S: What 'S' was more crafty than any other animal?

B: What 'B' was the land where the king gave Jehoiachin an allowance for as long as he lived?

N: What 'N' had a church in her house in Colosse?

M: What 'M' was the father of Samson?

H: What 'H' was flowing besides milk in Canaan?

O: What 'O' were stones to be mounted on the priest's ephod?

D: What 'D' is the end of the broad road?

L: What 'L' is the period leading up to Easter?

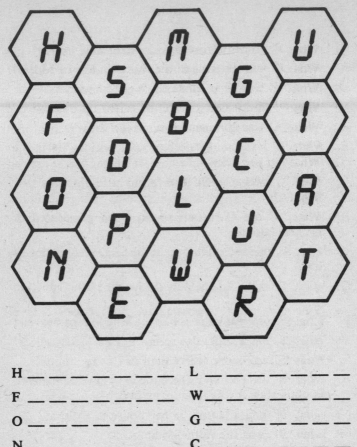

H _ _ _ _ _ _ _ _   L _ _ _ _ _ _ _

F _ _ _ _ _ _ _ _   W _ _ _ _ _ _ _

O _ _ _ _ _ _ _ _   G _ _ _ _ _ _ _

N _ _ _ _ _ _ _ _   C _ _ _ _ _ _ _

S _ _ _ _ _ _ _ _   J _ _ _ _ _ _ _

D _ _ _ _ _ _ _ _   R _ _ _ _ _ _ _

P _ _ _ _ _ _ _ _   U _ _ _ _ _ _ _

E _ _ _ _ _ _ _ _   I _ _ _ _ _ _ _

M _ _ _ _ _ _ _ _   A _ _ _ _ _ _ _

B _ _ _ _ _ _ _ _   T _ _ _ _ _ _ _

H: What 'H' did the people of Lystra call Paul?

F: What 'F' did Rahab use to cover the spies in Jericho?

O: What 'O' comes before cast, come and cry?

N: What 'N' was a mighty hunter before the Lord?

S: What 'S' struck down six hundred Philistines with an ox-goad?

D: What 'D' was the plain where Nebuchadnezzar erected a ninety-foot golden image?

P: What 'P' was a herd into which Jesus ordered demons?

E: What 'E' means 'thus far has the Lord helped us'?

M: What 'M' was King David's wife?

B: What 'B' is the overall name of eight special sayings of Jesus?

L: What 'L' was Timothy's grandmother?

W: What 'W' was an American president supposed never to have told a lie?

G: What 'G' was the region in Egypt where Jacob's household was allowed to settle?

C: What 'C' is a baby's naming ceremony in church?

J: What 'J' is the name of God from the Hebrew Yahwe?

R: What 'R' meaning teacher did Mary Magdalene exclaim when she saw the risen Jesus?

U: What 'U' comes before pass, fed and dog?

I: What 'I' was one boundary of the kingdom of Xerxes?

A: What 'A' was an Amalakite king whom Saul captured?

T: What 'T' presented Paul's case before Felix?

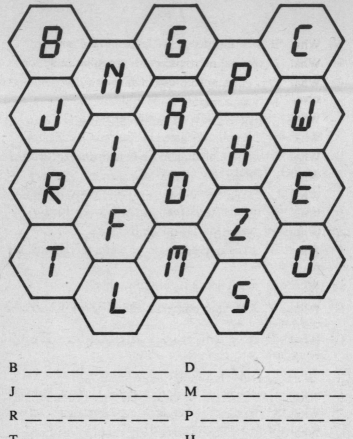

B _ _ _ _ _ _ _ _ _   D _ _ _ _ _ _ _ _ _

J _ _ _ _ _ _ _ _ _   M _ _ _ _ _ _ _ _ _

R _ _ _ _ _ _ _ _ _   P _ _ _ _ _ _ _ _ _

T _ _ _ _ _ _ _ _ _   H _ _ _ _ _ _ _ _ _

N _ _ _ _ _ _ _ _ _   Z _ _ _ _ _ _ _ _ _

I _ _ _ _ _ _ _ _ _   S _ _ _ _ _ _ _ _ _

F _ _ _ _ _ _ _ _ _   C _ _ _ _ _ _ _ _ _

L _ _ _ _ _ _ _ _ _   W _ _ _ _ _ _ _ _ _

G _ _ _ _ _ _ _ _ _   E _ _ _ _ _ _ _ _ _

A _ _ _ _ _ _ _ _ _   O _ _ _ _ _ _ _ _ _

18

B: What 'B' was murdered in Canterbury Cathedral?

J: What 'J' was a ford crossed by Jacob's family?

R: What 'R' according to Malachi sits purifying gold and silver?

T: What 'T' was the Herod in Luke's Gospel?

N: What 'N' had practices hated by the church in Ephesus?

I: What 'I' was the Christian name of hymnwriter Sankey?

F: What 'F' ruined the vineyards in Song of Songs?

L: What 'L' of the world are Christians expected to be?

G: What 'G' was a missionary doctor to Labrador?

A: What 'A' was a cave where David's brother found him?

D: What 'D' according to John's third letter loved to be first?

M: What 'M' was also named Levi?

P: What 'P' gave his name to the City of London's cathedral?

H: What 'H' meaning 'save' did the crowd cry on Palm Sunday?

Z: What 'Z' is the holy hill in Jerusalem?

S: What 'S' was the site of the temple where Eli served as priest?

C: What 'C' was where Jesus taught that he was Lord of the Sabbath?

W: What 'W' was the Christian name of Booth, the Founder of The Salvation Army?

E: What 'E' was the home of a witch visited by David?

O: What 'O' was remembered with leeks and garlic by the wandering Israelites?

O _ _ _ _ _ _ _ _   U _ _ _ _ _ _ _ _

C _ _ _ _ _ _ _ _   K _ _ _ _ _ _ _ _

D _ _ _ _ _ _ _ _   Z _ _ _ _ _ _ _ _

W _ _ _ _ _ _ _ _   Y _ _ _ _ _ _ _ _

M _ _ _ _ _ _ _ _   V _ _ _ _ _ _ _ _

N _ _ _ _ _ _ _ _   L _ _ _ _ _ _ _ _

E _ _ _ _ _ _ _ _   A _ _ _ _ _ _ _ _

G _ _ _ _ _ _ _ _   F _ _ _ _ _ _ _ _

H _ _ _ _ _ _ _ _   J _ _ _ _ _ _ _ _

T _ _ _ _ _ _ _ _   B _ _ _ _ _ _ _ _

O: What 'O' received special greetings in Paul's second letter to Timothy?

C: What 'C' is England's chief cathedral?

D: What 'D' was an armour-bearer before becoming king of Israel?

W: What 'W' was a John and converted on 24 May 1738?

M: What 'M' was the first word Belshazzar saw on the banquet hall wall?

N: What 'N' was the land where Cain lived?

E: What 'E' was given a scroll to eat when called to prophesy?

G: What 'G' comes before will, bye and Friday?

H: What 'H' deserted Paul in the province of Asia?

T: What 'T' must a Christian not worry about today?

U: What 'U' pairs with Thummin?

K: What 'K' must we do with any oath we make?

Z: What 'Z' was a prophet who had a vision of a flying scroll and a woman in a basket?

Y: What 'Y' works through the whole batch?

V: What 'V' did the King of Egypt's chief cupbearer see in a dream in prison?

L: What 'L' is a sorrowful Old Testament book attributed to Jeremiah?

A: What 'A' is the period leading up to Christmas?

F: What 'F' went out to sow his seed?

J: What 'J' was son of Mary and brother of James?

B: What 'B' did Nebuchadnezzar call Daniel?

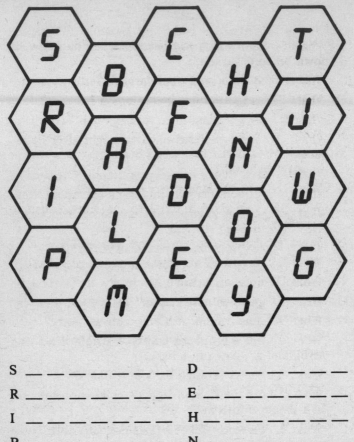

S _ _ _ _ _ _ _ _ _

R _ _ _ _ _ _ _ _ _

I _ _ _ _ _ _ _ _ _

P _ _ _ _ _ _ _ _ _

B _ _ _ _ _ _ _ _ _

A _ _ _ _ _ _ _ _ _

L _ _ _ _ _ _ _ _ _

M _ _ _ _ _ _ _ _ _

C _ _ _ _ _ _ _ _ _

F _ _ _ _ _ _ _ _ _

D _ _ _ _ _ _ _ _ _

E _ _ _ _ _ _ _ _ _

H _ _ _ _ _ _ _ _ _

N _ _ _ _ _ _ _ _ _

O _ _ _ _ _ _ _ _ _

Y _ _ _ _ _ _ _ _ _

T _ _ _ _ _ _ _ _ _

J _ _ _ _ _ _ _ _ _

W _ _ _ _ _ _ _ _ _

G _ _ _ _ _ _ _ _ _

S: What 'S' did Aaron's rod become when he threw it down before Pharaoh?

R: What 'R' did Noah send from the ark after forty days?

I: What 'I' was used in making Solomon's throne?

P: What 'P' has a leaning tower near its baptistry?

B: What 'B' was where Jesus spent the night after Palm Sunday?

A: What 'A' used Paul's belt to prophesy in Caesarea?

L: What 'L' was a chosen one in John's second epistle?

M: What 'M' is money given away by the Queen of England just before Easter?

C: What 'C' met Jesus on the Emmaus Road?

F: What 'F' was the place where Nebuchadnezzar threw the three Hebrew boys?

D: What 'D' did the disciples of Jesus find tied in Bethphage?

E: What 'E' issued by Xerxes gave Jews the right of assembly?

H: What 'H' was the worst storm in the days of Moses that Egypt had ever known?

N: What 'N' was a perfume used by Mary of Bethany?

O: What 'O' was the word Isaiah used for prophecy?

Y: What 'Y' was scarlet in the tabernacle curtains?

T: What 'T' was the son of Eunice?

J: What 'J' was the home of Tabitha?

W: What 'W' comes before draw, hold and stand?

G: What 'G' was the mount where King Saul died?

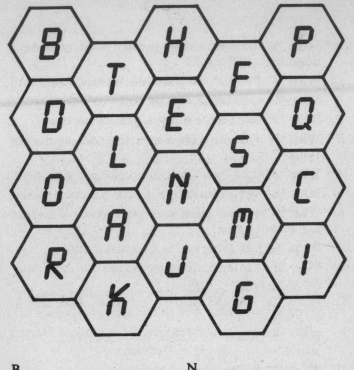

B _ _ _ _ _ _ _ _   N _ _ _ _ _ _ _
D _ _ _ _ _ _ _ _   J _ _ _ _ _ _ _
O _ _ _ _ _ _ _ _   F _ _ _ _ _ _ _
R _ _ _ _ _ _ _ _   S _ _ _ _ _ _ _
T _ _ _ _ _ _ _ _   M _ _ _ _ _ _ _
L _ _ _ _ _ _ _ _   G _ _ _ _ _ _ _
A _ _ _ _ _ _ _ _   P _ _ _ _ _ _ _
K _ _ _ _ _ _ _ _   Q _ _ _ _ _ _ _
H _ _ _ _ _ _ _ _   C _ _ _ _ _ _ _
E _ _ _ _ _ _ _ _   I _ _ _ _ _ _ _

B: What 'B' was the temple gate where Peter healed a cripple?

D: What 'D' returned to Noah with an olive leaf?

O: What 'O' must not be muzzled while it treads the grain?

R: What 'R' was Paul's stopping place after Cos?

T: What 'T' was a tree under which King Saul was buried?

L: What 'L' was an invasion predicted by Joel?

A: What 'A' was king in Jerusalem when Jesus was brought back from Egypt?

K: What 'K' was an unrepentant city Jesus denounced?

H: What 'H' was brother of Phinehas and son of Eli?

E: What 'E' will be done to a man who humbles himself?

N: What 'N' was father of King Jehu?

J: What 'J' is the shortest name of any Bible book?

F: What 'F' does God give to one who is repentant?

S: What 'S' was the commander of the army of Hazor?

M: What 'M' lost his ear in Gethsemane?

G: What 'G' was the wife of Hosea?

P: What 'P' did Jesus say he would prepare for his disciples?

Q: What 'Q' is a Christian society founded by George Fox in the seventeenth century?

C: What 'C' is a vicar's full-time assistant?

I: What 'I' was a prophet John the Baptist quoted in the desert?

F _ _ _ _ _ _ _ P _ _ _ _ _ _ _
K _ _ _ _ _ _ _ T _ _ _ _ _ _ _
U _ _ _ _ _ _ _ S _ _ _ _ _ _ _
V _ _ _ _ _ _ _ B _ _ _ _ _ _ _
A _ _ _ _ _ _ _ N _ _ _ _ _ _ _
E _ _ _ _ _ _ _ M _ _ _ _ _ _ _
C _ _ _ _ _ _ _ H _ _ _ _ _ _ _
R _ _ _ _ _ _ _ O _ _ _ _ _ _ _
I _ _ _ _ _ _ _ D _ _ _ _ _ _ _
G _ _ _ _ _ _ _ L _ _ _ _ _ _ _

F: What 'F' was one of Assisi's greatest sons?

K: What 'K' was Paul's port of call after Mitylene?

U: What 'U' is a warrior buried in Westminster Abbey?

V: What 'V' are the official garments of the clergy?

A: What 'A' died and made David cry: 'O my son!'?

E: What 'E' is another name for the Lord's Supper?

C: What 'C' besides psalms and hymns are sung in church services?

R: What 'R' with the sower is glad at harvest?

I: What 'I' was a boy whose name meant 'the glory has departed from Israel'?

G: What 'G' was the landing place for Jesus after he had walked on water?

P: What 'P' holds the highest office in the Roman Catholic Church?

T: What 'T' comes usually at night?

S: What 'S' did Jehoiakim burn belonging to Jeremiah?

B: What 'B' in the parable did the ten virgins go out to meet?

N: What 'N' did Jesus see sitting under a fig-tree?

M: What 'M' took the place of Judas among the apostles?

H: What 'H' was a queen supposed to have found the real cross of Jesus?

O: What 'O' is an Old Testament prophecy with only twenty-one verses?

D: What 'D' represented the Spirit of God at the baptism of Jesus?

L: What 'L' comes after Bread of, eternal and Light of?

H _ _ _ _ _ _ _ _   L _ _ _ _ _ _ _

F _ _ _ _ _ _ _ _   W _ _ _ _ _ _ _

O _ _ _ _ _ _ _ _   G _ _ _ _ _ _ _

N _ _ _ _ _ _ _ _   C _ _ _ _ _ _ _

S _ _ _ _ _ _ _ _   J _ _ _ _ _ _ _

D _ _ _ _ _ _ _ _   R _ _ _ _ _ _ _

P _ _ _ _ _ _ _ _   U _ _ _ _ _ _ _

E _ _ _ _ _ _ _ _   I _ _ _ _ _ _ _

M _ _ _ _ _ _ _ _   A _ _ _ _ _ _ _

B _ _ _ _ _ _ _ _   T _ _ _ _ _ _ _

H: What 'H' comes before Spirit, City and One?

F: What 'F' is going without food?

O: What 'O' is the last letter of the Greek alphabet?

N: What 'N' was good and brought by the Bethlehem angels to the shepherds?

S: What 'S' was sent to find David Livingstone in Africa?

D: What 'D' could be cancelled at the end of seven years according to the Mosaic law?

P: What 'P' is a Bible term for the father of a family or tribe?

E: What 'E' was the camp of the Israelites when their ark was captured?

M: What 'M' was the district where in a vision Paul was called to come and help?

B: What 'B' took dictation from Jeremiah?

L: What 'L' comes before sheep, coin and son?

W: What 'W' successfully worked for the abolition of slavery in the British Empire?

G: What 'G' will be on his left when the Son of Man comes in his glory?

C: What 'C' was an animal which provided John the Baptist's clothing?

J: What 'J' was son of Saul?

R: What 'R' was the son of Jacob and Leah?

U: What 'U' was the archbishop who added dates to the Bible?

I: What 'I' was made King of Israel when Saul died?

A: What 'A' of Jesus did the chief priests question in the temple courts?

T: What 'T' was the third river flowing from Eden?

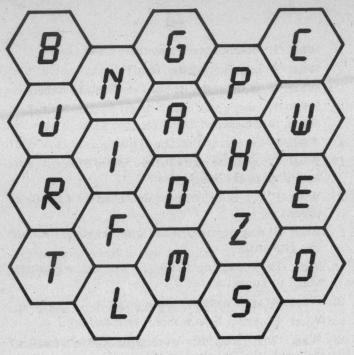

B _ _ _ _ _ _ _ _   D _ _ _ _ _ _ _
J _ _ _ _ _ _ _ _   M _ _ _ _ _ _ _
R _ _ _ _ _ _ _ _   P _ _ _ _ _ _ _
T _ _ _ _ _ _ _ _   H _ _ _ _ _ _ _
N _ _ _ _ _ _ _ _   Z _ _ _ _ _ _ _
I _ _ _ _ _ _ _ _   S _ _ _ _ _ _ _
F _ _ _ _ _ _ _ _   C _ _ _ _ _ _ _
L _ _ _ _ _ _ _ _   W _ _ _ _ _ _ _
G _ _ _ _ _ _ _ _   E _ _ _ _ _ _ _
A _ _ _ _ _ _ _ _   O _ _ _ _ _ _ _

B: What 'B' was Solomon's mother?

J: What 'J' had a daughter Jesus brought back to life?

R: What 'R' did the Son of Man give his life to become for many?

T: What 'T' translated the Bible into English and was executed?

N: What 'N' is a child given when christened?

I: What 'I' means undying?

F: What 'F' comes before of righteousness, of the Spirit and of the vine?

L: What 'L' was the material of John the Baptist's belt?

G: What 'G' comes before shepherd, news and works?

A: What 'A' was a Jebusite on whose threshing floor David built an altar?

D: What 'D' was an idol which fell before the ark of the Lord?

M: What 'M' was a Cypriot who housed Paul in Jerusalem?

P: What 'P' asked Jesus: 'What is truth?'?

H: What 'H' was the place of David's anointing as King of Israel?

Z: What 'Z' was a lawyer whom Paul asked Titus to remember needed help?

S: What 'S' was Adam's third son?

C: What 'C' is a Derbyshire Methodist training college?

W: What 'W' did the early Christians belong to?

E: What 'E' was another name for Bar-Jesus the sorcerer?

O: What 'O' was a Christian philosopher who died in AD 254?

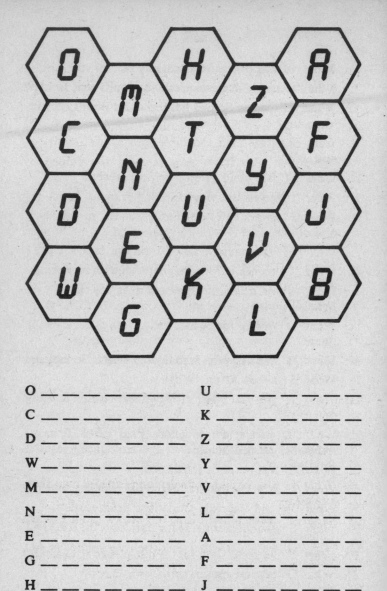

O _ _ _ _ _ _ _ _   U _ _ _ _ _ _ _ _

C _ _ _ _ _ _ _ _   K _ _ _ _ _ _ _ _

D _ _ _ _ _ _ _ _   Z _ _ _ _ _ _ _ _

W _ _ _ _ _ _ _ _   Y _ _ _ _ _ _ _ _

M _ _ _ _ _ _ _ _   V _ _ _ _ _ _ _ _

N _ _ _ _ _ _ _ _   L _ _ _ _ _ _ _ _

E _ _ _ _ _ _ _ _   A _ _ _ _ _ _ _ _

G _ _ _ _ _ _ _ _   F _ _ _ _ _ _ _ _

H _ _ _ _ _ _ _ _   J _ _ _ _ _ _ _ _

T _ _ _ _ _ _ _ _   B _ _ _ _ _ _ _ _

25

O: What 'O' introduced Christianity to Northumbria?

C: What 'C' did Jesus have on two blind men near Jericho?

D: What 'D' comes before fall, cast and pour?

W: What 'W' is a gallery beneath the dome of St. Paul's Cathedral?

M: What 'M' was Jonathan's crippled son helped by David?

N: What 'N' was the time Elijah began to tempt the prophets of Baal on Carmel?

E: What 'E' is a Bedfordshire village where John Bunyan was born in 1628?

G: What 'G' is the colour associated with old age?

H: What 'H' painted 'The Light of the World'?

T: What 'T' had to be paid to Caesar throughout the Roman Empire?

U: What 'U' comes before rooted, hold and set?

K: What 'K' was a river in Babylon where Ezekiel saw visions?

Z: What 'Z' was the priest when the people shouted: 'Long live King Solomon'?

Y: What 'Y' goes with today and for ever?

V: What 'V' came from heaven and announced Jesus as God's Son?

L: What 'L' was the name of a demon-possessed man Jesus healed?

A: What 'A' made himself King of Israel without David's knowledge?

F: What 'F' did Jesus wash for the disciples as an example?

J: What 'J' became one in spirit with David?

B: What 'B' was a Cypriot whose name means 'Son of encouragement'?

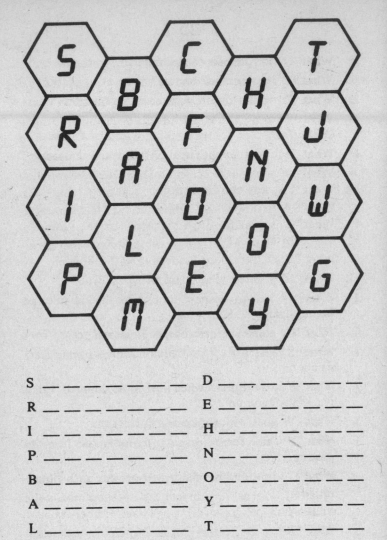

S _ _ _ _ _ _ _ _   D _ _ _ _ _ _ _
R _ _ _ _ _ _ _ _   E _ _ _ _ _ _ _
I _ _ _ _ _ _ _ _   H _ _ _ _ _ _ _
P _ _ _ _ _ _ _ _   N _ _ _ _ _ _ _
B _ _ _ _ _ _ _ _   O _ _ _ _ _ _ _
A _ _ _ _ _ _ _ _   Y _ _ _ _ _ _ _
L _ _ _ _ _ _ _ _   T _ _ _ _ _ _ _
M _ _ _ _ _ _ _ _   J _ _ _ _ _ _ _
C _ _ _ _ _ _ _ _   W _ _ _ _ _ _ _
F _ _ _ _ _ _ _ _   G _ _ _ _ _ _ _

26

S: What 'S' was Peter's earlier name?

R: What 'R' was Samuel's home?

I: What 'I' was the Christian name of hymnwriters Watts and Newton?

P: What 'P' comes before of Siloam and of Gibeon?

B: What 'B' filled a valley and gave Ezekiel a message?

A: What 'A' were in Jerusalem on the Day of Pentecost and are now a powerful race?

L: What 'L' is an animal known for its unchangeable spots?

M: What 'M' was under the care of Judas in the group of apostles?

C: What 'C' is a clanging instrument?

F: What 'F' overcame Peter's mother-in-law in Capernaum?

D: What 'D' was the type of heart Solomon prayed for?

E: What 'E' fell from a third-storey window during Paul's sermon?

H: What 'H' was the shrivelled part of a man healed in a synagogue?

N: What 'N' is the fourth book of the Bible?

O: What 'O' did James urge us to look after besides widows?

Y: What 'Y' in a parable did a woman mix with flour?

T: What 'T' was the worship tent the Israelites used in the wilderness?

J: What 'J' was the King of England when the Authorised Version of the Bible was published?

W: What 'W' is a title for Jesus in John's Gospel?

G: What 'G' was a Macedonian who was arrested in a riot in Ephesus?

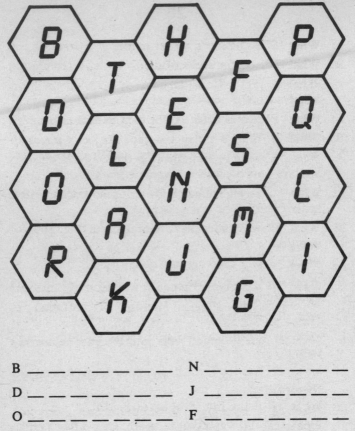

B _ _ _ _ _ _ _ _   N _ _ _ _ _ _ _ _
D _ _ _ _ _ _ _ _   J _ _ _ _ _ _ _ _
O _ _ _ _ _ _ _ _   F _ _ _ _ _ _ _ _
R _ _ _ _ _ _ _ _   S _ _ _ _ _ _ _ _
T _ _ _ _ _ _ _ _   M _ _ _ _ _ _ _ _
L _ _ _ _ _ _ _ _   G _ _ _ _ _ _ _ _
A _ _ _ _ _ _ _ _   P _ _ _ _ _ _ _ _
K _ _ _ _ _ _ _ _   Q _ _ _ _ _ _ _ _
H _ _ _ _ _ _ _ _   C _ _ _ _ _ _ _ _
E _ _ _ _ _ _ _ _   I _ _ _ _ _ _ _ _

27

B: What 'B' is the blessing at the end of a service?

D: What 'D' was the scene of the forty days' temptation of Jesus?

O: What 'O' is the main musical instrument in a church?

R: What 'R' did God set in the clouds as a sign of his covenant with Noah?

T: What 'T' lived in Lystra of Jewish and Greek parentage?

L: What 'L' was John the Baptist's main food?

A: What 'A' was the town of Philip's reappearance after leaving the Ethiopian eunuch?

K: What 'K' did Judas use to betray Jesus?

H: What 'H' is another term for hell?

E: What 'E' is a New Testament epistle?

N: What 'N' was another name for Simeon of Antioch?

J: What 'J' was dragged before city officials in Thessalonica?

F: What 'F' were Peter and three more disciples before they followed Jesus?

S: What 'S' was denied the Israelites when they made bricks in Egypt?

M: What 'M' was the Mary to whom the risen Jesus first appeared?

G: What 'G' are insects likened to an uncountable number?

P: What 'P' broke out in Jerusalem the day Stephen was stoned?

Q: What 'Q' sent greetings in Paul's letter to the Romans?

C: What 'C' crowed when Peter denied Jesus?

I: What 'I' is missing from 'Immortal . . . God only wise'?

F _ _ _ _ _ _ _ _   P _ _ _ _ _ _ _
K _ _ _ _ _ _ _ _   T _ _ _ _ _ _ _
U _ _ _ _ _ _ _ _   S _ _ _ _ _ _ _
V _ _ _ _ _ _ _ _   B _ _ _ _ _ _ _
A _ _ _ _ _ _ _ _   N _ _ _ _ _ _ _
E _ _ _ _ _ _ _ _   M _ _ _ _ _ _ _
C _ _ _ _ _ _ _ _   H _ _ _ _ _ _ _
R _ _ _ _ _ _ _ _   O _ _ _ _ _ _ _
I _ _ _ _ _ _ _ _   D _ _ _ _ _ _ _
G _ _ _ _ _ _ _ _   L _ _ _ _ _ _ _

28

F: What 'F' is the place of a baby's christening?

K: What 'K' is a brotherly quality to be added to godliness?

U: What 'U' has not accepted the Christian faith?

V: What 'V' is a period of night-time devotions?

A: What 'A' was a city where Paul met a group of Epicureans?

E: What 'E' is a preacher of the Gospel?

C: What 'C' of cardinals meet to elect a Pope?

R: What 'R' was the citizenship claimed by Paul and Silas?

I: What 'I' was the blood betrayed by Judas?

G: What 'G' was a Pope who sent Augustine to England?

P: What 'P' was a Roman colony where Paul and Silas were imprisoned?

T: What 'T' was the home of a demon-possessed man before Jesus met him?

S: What 'S' was the number of years Solomon took to build the Jerusalem temple?

B: What 'B' was Paul not allowed by the Spirit of Jesus to enter?

N: What 'N' is how often God will forsake his people?

M: What 'M' was brought up with Herod the Tetrarch?

H: What 'H' is the time of year when grain is ripe?

O: What 'O' is the habitation of great sea creatures?

D: What 'D' was the road where Paul was converted?

L: What 'L' pitched his tents near Sodom?

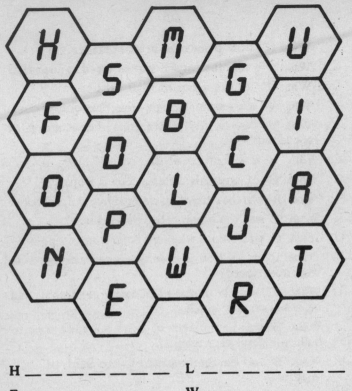

H _ _ _ _ _ _ _   L _ _ _ _ _ _ _

F _ _ _ _ _ _ _   W _ _ _ _ _ _ _

O _ _ _ _ _ _ _   G _ _ _ _ _ _ _

N _ _ _ _ _ _ _   C _ _ _ _ _ _ _

S _ _ _ _ _ _ _   J _ _ _ _ _ _ _

D _ _ _ _ _ _ _   R _ _ _ _ _ _ _

P _ _ _ _ _ _ _   U _ _ _ _ _ _ _

E _ _ _ _ _ _ _   I _ _ _ _ _ _ _

M _ _ _ _ _ _ _   A _ _ _ _ _ _ _

B _ _ _ _ _ _ _   T _ _ _ _ _ _ _

29

H: What 'H' is the final abode of wicked?

F: What 'F' does the ostrich spread when she runs?

O: What 'O' is a religious musical work?

N: What 'N' is a good thing even better than fine perfume?

S: What 'S' was a valley full of tarpits in Abraham's day?

D: What 'D' flew open in Paul's Philippian jail?

P: What 'P' was the town Paul visited next after Paphos?

E: What 'E' disagreed with Syntyche in Philippi?

M: What 'M' is Christ between God and men?

B: What 'B' was a field bought with the betrayal money of Jesus?

L: What 'L' was the source of cedar and pine for Solomon's temple?

W: What 'W' is our purpose in going to church?

G: What 'G' was a theologian and four times British Prime Minister?

C: What 'C' were only a few of those who in the parable had been invited to the wedding banquet?

J: What 'J' was a prophet who when he was called felt he was only a child?

R: What 'R' is the side the sheep will stand when the Son of Man comes in his glory?

U: What 'U' comes before lawful, mindful and seen?

I: What 'I' did Baruch use when writing Jeremiah's scroll?

A: What 'A' was the father of Isaiah?

T: What 'T' accompanied the plague of hail in Egypt?

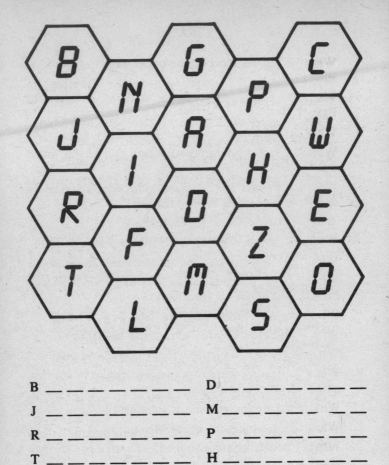

B _ _ _ _ _ _ _ _   D _ _ _ _ _ _ _
J _ _ _ _ _ _ _ _   M _ _ _ _ _ _ _
R _ _ _ _ _ _ _ _   P _ _ _ _ _ _ _
T _ _ _ _ _ _ _ _   H _ _ _ _ _ _ _
N _ _ _ _ _ _ _ _   Z _ _ _ _ _ _ _
I _ _ _ _ _ _ _ _   S _ _ _ _ _ _ _
F _ _ _ _ _ _ _ _   C _ _ _ _ _ _ _
L _ _ _ _ _ _ _ _   W _ _ _ _ _ _ _
G _ _ _ _ _ _ _ _   E _ _ _ _ _ _ _
A _ _ _ _ _ _ _ _   O _ _ _ _ _ _ _

30

B: What 'B' mauled forty-two youths who had jeered at Elisha?

J: What 'J' rose suddenly from slave to governor of Egypt?

R: What 'R' did the church in Laodicea falsely claim to be?

T: What 'T' on Belshazzar's wall meant that he was found wanting?

N: What 'N' was the true relationship between a Samaritan and a man who fell among thieves?

I: What 'I' is another word for idols?

F: What 'F' is produced at the beginning of harvest?

L: What 'L' describes the Simon who lived in Bethany?

G: What 'G' was an arranged meeting place for Jesus and his disciples after his resurrection?

A: What 'A' is a Wednesday, the first day of Lent?

D: What 'D' comes before light, break and time?

M: What 'M' was too worried about household matters?

P: What 'P' was a workman whom Jeremiah saw making an object the second time?

H: What 'H' was the mother of Ishmael?

Z: What 'Z' is the desert where Miriam died?

S: What 'S' did Elisha use to purify a spring in Jericho?

C: What 'C' were disciples first called in Antioch?

W: What 'W' is the Sunday when we celebrate Pentecost?

E: What 'E' was a precious stone on the priest's breastpiece?

O: What 'O' is a constellation mentioned in the Book of Job?

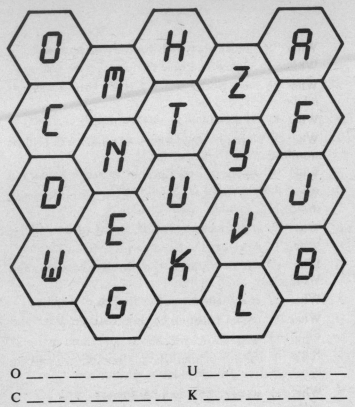

O _ _ _ _ _ _ _ _   U _ _ _ _ _ _

C _ _ _ _ _ _ _ _   K _ _ _ _ _ _

D _ _ _ _ _ _ _ _   Z _ _ _ _ _ _

W _ _ _ _ _ _ _ _   Y _ _ _ _ _ _

M _ _ _ _ _ _ _ _   V _ _ _ _ _ _

N _ _ _ _ _ _ _ _   L _ _ _ _ _ _

E _ _ _ _ _ _ _ _   A _ _ _ _ _ _

G _ _ _ _ _ _ _ _   F _ _ _ _ _ _

H _ _ _ _ _ _ _ _   J _ _ _ _ _ _

T _ _ _ _ _ _ _ _   B _ _ _ _ _ _

31

O: What 'O' did the disciples strain at in the boat?

C: What 'C' reigned in Rome during a severe famine?

D: What 'D' were paid when in Elisha's time a widow's oil flowed on and on?

W: What 'W' is a watercourse which often runs dry?

M: What 'M' was the place where Abraham was told he would become a great nation?

N: What 'N' was a man of Carmel?

E: What 'E' is an Old Testament book written by Solomon the Teacher?

G: What 'G' did Solomon use to cover the inside of his temple?

H: What 'H' was the transport generally used by John Wesley?

T: What 'T' is another name for the Sea of Galilee?

U: What 'U' had Onesimus become to both Paul and Philemon?

K: What 'K' was the ravine where the ravens fed Elijah?

Z: What 'Z' was a Bible musical instrument?

Y: What 'Y' according to Joel are the men who will see visions?

V: What 'V' is the poisonous fluid of serpents?

L: What 'L' must a man be if he wants to be first?

A: What 'A' predicted a famine in the Roman world?

F: What 'F' did Jeremiah buy from Hanamel in Anathoth?

J: What 'J' hanged himself after he had betrayed Jesus?

B: What 'B' did the Stoics in Athens call Paul?

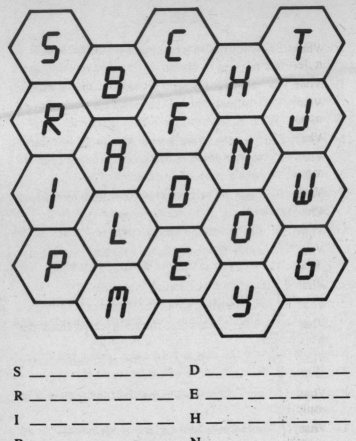

S _ _ _ _ _ _ _ _ _

R _ _ _ _ _ _ _ _

I _ _ _ _ _ _ _ _

P _ _ _ _ _ _ _ _

B _ _ _ _ _ _ _ _

A _ _ _ _ _ _ _ _

L _ _ _ _ _ _ _ _

M _ _ _ _ _ _ _ _

C _ _ _ _ _ _ _ _

F _ _ _ _ _ _ _ _

D _ _ _ _ _ _ _ _

E _ _ _ _ _ _ _ _

H _ _ _ _ _ _ _ _

N _ _ _ _ _ _ _ _

O _ _ _ _ _ _ _ _

Y _ _ _ _ _ _ _ _

T _ _ _ _ _ _ _ _

J _ _ _ _ _ _ _ _

W _ _ _ _ _ _ _ _

G _ _ _ _ _ _ _ _

32

S: What 'S' was the queen's country who visited Solomon in Jerusalem?

R: What 'R' was a family who would not drink wine?

I: What 'I' is a horned animal the Israelites were allowed to eat?

P: What 'P' is a type of song used in church worship?

B: What 'B' was a murderer the crowd wanted released instead of Jesus?

A: What 'A' was a jar of perfume used in Bethany?

L: What 'L' were the followers of John Wycliffe?

M: What 'M' was the first bed for Jesus?

C: What 'C' was the home of Simon who carried the cross for Jesus?

F: What 'F' is a Bible woodwind instrument?

D: What 'D' was another name for Thomas?

E: What 'E' was the road where the resurrected Jesus met two disciples?

H: What 'H' was the shout of the multitude in the Revelation?

N: What 'N' were the marks Thomas had to see before he would believe?

O: What 'O' was a tree where Gideon made a meal for an angel?

Y: What 'Y' were Stephen's murderers doing as they dragged him to stoning?

T: What 'T' was the number of silver coins with which Judas sold Jesus?

J: What 'J' is the fiftieth year?

W: What 'W' of sin is death?

G: What 'G' was the garden where Jesus was arrested?

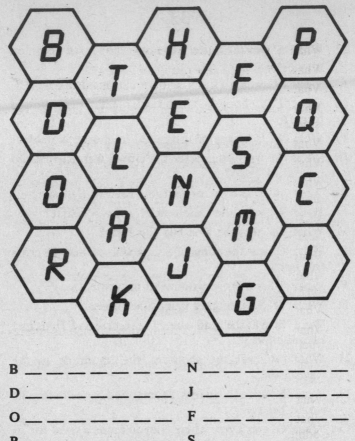

B _ _ _ _ _ _ _ _ _   N _ _ _ _ _ _ _ _
D _ _ _ _ _ _ _ _ _   J _ _ _ _ _ _ _ _
O _ _ _ _ _ _ _ _ _   F _ _ _ _ _ _ _ _
R _ _ _ _ _ _ _ _ _   S _ _ _ _ _ _ _ _
T _ _ _ _ _ _ _ _ _   M _ _ _ _ _ _ _ _
L _ _ _ _ _ _ _ _ _   G _ _ _ _ _ _ _ _
A _ _ _ _ _ _ _ _ _   P _ _ _ _ _ _ _ _
K _ _ _ _ _ _ _ _ _   Q _ _ _ _ _ _ _ _
H _ _ _ _ _ _ _ _ _   C _ _ _ _ _ _ _ _
E _ _ _ _ _ _ _ _ _   I _ _ _ _ _ _ _ _

33

B: What 'B' was Gilead well known for?

D: What 'D' is the patron saint of Wales?

O: What 'O' comes before shoots, set and spring?

R: What 'R' was the sea which became dry land for the Israelites?

T: What 'T' made up the cross worn by Jesus?

L: What 'L' was a Passover sacrificial offering?

A: What 'A' is the first letter of the Greek alphabet?

K: What 'K' of the kingdom were given to Peter?

H: What 'H' was a prophet associated with Jerusalem's second temple?

E: What 'E' was Naomi's husband?

N: What 'N' was a town where Jesus resurrected a widow's son?

J: What 'J' was a son of Noah?

F: What 'F' was the cruelty Pilate ordered for Jesus before crucifixion?

S: What 'S' was the home of a widow whose son Elisha restored to life?

M: What 'M' is the headwear of a bishop?

G: What 'G' was the city Abraham prayed for other than Sodom?

P: What 'P' was a lofty height with Nebo as its summit?

Q: What 'Q' was the office held by Candace of Ethiopia?

C: What 'C' besides Comforter is a title for the Holy Spirit?

I: What 'I' was to Ezekiel sparkling and awesome?

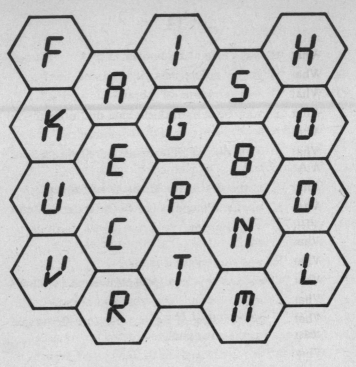

F _ _ _ _ _ _ _ _ _   P _ _ _ _ _ _ _

K _ _ _ _ _ _ _ _   T _ _ _ _ _ _ _

U _ _ _ _ _ _ _ _   S _ _ _ _ _ _ _

V _ _ _ _ _ _ _ _   B _ _ _ _ _ _ _

A _ _ _ _ _ _ _ _   N _ _ _ _ _ _ _

E _ _ _ _ _ _ _ _   M _ _ _ _ _ _ _

C _ _ _ _ _ _ _ _   H _ _ _ _ _ _ _

R _ _ _ _ _ _ _ _   O _ _ _ _ _ _ _

I _ _ _ _ _ _ _ _   D _ _ _ _ _ _ _

G _ _ _ _ _ _ _ _   L _ _ _ _ _ _ _

34

F: What 'F' is an animal Jesus likened to King Herod?

K: What 'K' comes before ness, hearted and ling?

U: What 'U' was the home of Abraham?

V: What 'V' were seen by Daniel, Paul and others?

A: What 'A' was the first man to be murdered?

E: What 'E' was a type of philosopher paired with a Stoic in Athens?

C: What 'C' is greatest in the kingdom of heaven?

R: What 'R' was the title Judas used as he spoke to Jesus during the Last Supper?

I: What 'I' was burned on an Israelite's altar?

G: What 'G' was a servant of Elisha?

P: What 'P' was a story Jesus told to illustrate a truth?

T: What 'T' comes before light, vine and bread?

S: What 'S' was the King of Egypt who stole the temple treasures from Rehoboam?

B: What 'B' was a name given to James and John?

N: What 'N' were desert wanderers?

M: What 'M' was a fruit the Israelites specially remembered from Egypt?

H: What 'H' describes Joseph's appearance?

O: What 'O' was the mount the disciples went to after the Last Supper?

D: What 'D' was a bronze Roman coin?

L: What 'L' was a plague in Egypt that left nothing green on any tree or plant?

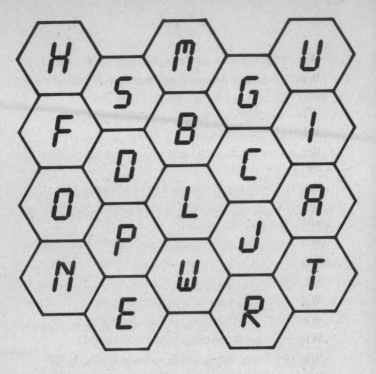

H _ _ _ _ _ _ _ _   L _ _ _ _ _ _ _
F _ _ _ _ _ _ _ _   W _ _ _ _ _ _ _ _
O _ _ _ _ _ _ _ _   G _ _ _ _ _ _ _
N _ _ _ _ _ _ _ _   C _ _ _ _ _ _ _ _
S _ _ _ _ _ _ _ _   J _ _ _ _ _ _ _
D _ _ _ _ _ _ _ _   R _ _ _ _ _ _ _ _
P _ _ _ _ _ _ _ _   U _ _ _ _ _ _ _
E _ _ _ _ _ _ _ _   I _ _ _ _ _ _ _ _
M _ _ _ _ _ _ _ _   A _ _ _ _ _ _ _
B _ _ _ _ _ _ _ _   T _ _ _ _ _ _ _

35

H: What 'H' became Lot's father and died in Ur?

F: What 'F' did Elisha put into a poisoned pot of stew to purify it?

O: What 'O' is admission to church ministry?

N: What 'N' was Elimelech's wife?

S: What 'S' was the name given to one of the Hebrew boys by Nebuchadnezzar?

D: What 'D' is sometimes called a wilderness?

P: What 'P' is a Jewish celebration established immediately after the plagues in Egypt?

E: What 'E' was a violent one on Easter morning?

M: What 'M' is linked with the Persians in Daniel's day?

B: What 'B' shall we find on the waters after many days?

L: What 'L' was a hungry beggar covered with sores?

W: What 'W' is a famous wall in Jerusalem?

G: What 'G' is the patron saint of England?

C: What 'C' was the synagogue ruler in Corinth?

J: What 'J' is a jewel linked with chrysolite and onyx?

R: What 'R' fed Elikah in the Kerith Ravine?

U: What 'U' had a brother called Buz?

I: What 'I' is passed on from father to son?

A: What 'A' was the father of the Hebrew race?

T: What 'T' was Paul's home town?

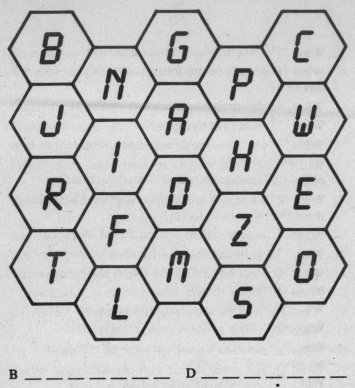

B _ _ _ _ _ _ _ _   D _ _ _ _ _ _ _ _

J _ _ _ _ _ _ _ _   M _ _ _ _ _ _ _ _

R _ _ _ _ _ _ _ _   P _ _ _ _ _ _ _ _

T _ _ _ _ _ _ _ _   H _ _ _ _ _ _ _ _

N _ _ _ _ _ _ _ _   Z _ _ _ _ _ _ _ _

I _ _ _ _ _ _ _ _   S _ _ _ _ _ _ _ _

F _ _ _ _ _ _ _ _   C _ _ _ _ _ _ _ _

L _ _ _ _ _ _ _ _   W _ _ _ _ _ _ _ _

G _ _ _ _ _ _ _ _   E _ _ _ _ _ _ _ _

A _ _ _ _ _ _ _ _   O _ _ _ _ _ _ _ _

36

B: What 'B' was a false god with an altar built on Carmel?

J: What 'J' is a city in the Jordan valley whose walls fell down?

R: What 'R' was an elegant one put on the arrested Jesus?

T: What 'T' wrote Paul's letter for him to the Romans?

N: What 'N' was a household who sent greetings to Rome?

I: What 'I' was a city where Paul discovered a murderous plot and escaped?

F: What 'F' was a pillar which led the Israelites through the night?

L: What 'L' should never be lit and put under a bowl?

G: What 'G' means the place of a skull?

A: What 'A' was a high priest when John the Baptist began his ministry?

D: What 'D' was the name of a group of ten cities?

M: What 'M' was a prophet born in Moresheth?

P: What 'P' was where Paul spent a week with friends on his journey to Rome?

H: What 'H' is a stringed instrument?

Z: What 'Z' was the home of a widow who gave Elijah a bread cake?

S: What 'S' was Jesus tempted to make into bread?

C: What 'C' did Paul appeal to for judgment?

W: What 'W' were brought to the gates of Lystra to honour Paul and Barnabas?

E: What 'E' was the first convert in the province of Asia?

O: What 'O' is another word for decrees?

O _ _ _ _ _ _ _   U _ _ _ _ _ _ _

C _ _ _ _ _ _ _   K _ _ _ _ _ _ _

D _ _ _ _ _ _ _   Z _ _ _ _ _ _ _

W _ _ _ _ _ _ _   Y _ _ _ _ _ _ _

M _ _ _ _ _ _ _   V _ _ _ _ _ _ _

N _ _ _ _ _ _ _   L _ _ _ _ _ _ _

E _ _ _ _ _ _ _   A _ _ _ _ _ _ _

G _ _ _ _ _ _ _   F _ _ _ _ _ _ _

H _ _ _ _ _ _ _   J _ _ _ _ _ _ _

T _ _ _ _ _ _ _   B _ _ _ _ _ _ _

37

O: What 'O' must we not put in our brother's way?

C: What 'C' appeared on Carmel as small as man's hand?

D: What 'D' comes before ease, cover and play?

W: What 'W' besides wind obeyed Jesus on the lake?

M: What 'M' was the region where Abraham prepared to offer Isaac as a sacrifice?

N: What 'N' was a prophet in David's time?

E: What 'E' was the younger son of Joseph?

G: What 'G' were reprimanded by Paul for their foolishness?

H: What 'H' was the number of men Elisha fed with twenty barley loaves?

T: What 'T' broke open at the death of Jesus?

U: What 'U' is a military group or one piece?

K: What 'K' is the name of two Old Testament books?

Z: What 'Z' did Lot flee to and thus avoid destruction?

Y: What 'Y' in wages was the value of Mary of Bethany's perfume?

V: What 'V' is a solemn promise?

L: What 'L' was a town Peter visited near Joppa?

A: What 'A' gave Peter away when he denied his Lord?

F: What 'F' is a baby donkey?

J: What 'J' was father of King David?

B: What 'B' is an English town where the main church is known as 'the stump'?

S _ _ _ _ _ _ _   D _ _ _ _ _ _ _

R _ _ _ _ _ _ _   E _ _ _ _ _ _ _

I _ _ _ _ _ _ _   H _ _ _ _ _ _ _

P _ _ _ _ _ _ _   N _ _ _ _ _ _ _

B _ _ _ _ _ _ _   O _ _ _ _ _ _ _

A _ _ _ _ _ _ _   Y _ _ _ _ _ _ _

L _ _ _ _ _ _ _   T _ _ _ _ _ _ _

M _ _ _ _ _ _ _   J _ _ _ _ _ _ _

C _ _ _ _ _ _ _   W _ _ _ _ _ _ _

F _ _ _ _ _ _ _   G _ _ _ _ _ _ _

38

S: What 'S' were buildings where Jesus taught in Galilee?

R: What 'R' was a servant girl who heard Peter knocking at a door in Jerusalem?

I: What 'I' is a teacher?

P: What 'P' is Solomon famous for?

B: What 'B' was a blind man of Jericho?

A: What 'A' is the patron saint of Scotland?

L: What 'L' was a disease cured when Naaman dipped in Jordan?

M: What 'M' was king of Salem and a high priest?

C: What 'C' did Peter find in the mouth of a fish?

F: What 'F' is an enemy?

D: What 'D' is Christian belief and must be sound?

E: What 'E' shook when Jesus died?

H: What 'H' was a king of Aram anointed by Elijah?

N: What 'N' was the last mountain climbed by Moses?

O: What 'O' was father of Ahab?

Y: What 'Y' are the days in which we are exhorted to remember our creator?

T: What 'T' was another name for Dorcas?

J: What 'J' was preserved in a great fish?

W: What 'W' melts before the fire?

G: What 'G' was the road where Philip met the Ethiopian eunuch?

B _ _ _ _ _ _ _ _   N _ _ _ _ _ _ _

D _ _ _ _ _ _ _ _   J _ _ _ _ _ _ _

O _ _ _ _ _ _ _ _   F _ _ _ _ _ _ _

R _ _ _ _ _ _ _ _   S _ _ _ _ _ _ _

T _ _ _ _ _ _ _ _   M _ _ _ _ _ _ _

L _ _ _ _ _ _ _ _   G _ _ _ _ _ _ _

A _ _ _ _ _ _ _ _   P _ _ _ _ _ _ _

K _ _ _ _ _ _ _ _   Q _ _ _ _ _ _ _

H _ _ _ _ _ _ _ _   C _ _ _ _ _ _ _

E _ _ _ _ _ _ _ _   I _ _ _ _ _ _ _

39

B: What 'B' had a donkey which spoke to him?

D: What 'D' was visited by Paul immediately after Lystra?

O: What 'O' were the Jews to do with the Sabbath?

R: What 'R' is the foundation of a house that withstands the storm?

T: What 'T' was the city where Jason lived?

L: What 'L' was confused at Babel?

A: What 'A' was the valley where the sun stopped for a full day in Joshua's time?

K: What 'K' was the valley where Elijah killed the prophets of Baal?

H: What 'H' was the last king of Israel?

E: What 'E' are New Testament letters?

N: What 'N' housed birds although Jesus had nowhere to sleep?

J: What 'J' became king of Judah when he was eight?

F: What 'F' comes before step, print and stool?

S: What 'S' of the earth are Christians expected to be?

M: What 'M' is an eater of garments?

G: What 'G' is an English cathedral finished in 1965?

P: What 'P' was where Paul planned to winter in his voyage to Rome?

Q: What 'Q' was the boy Jesus asking the temple teachers?

C: What 'C' had the rich young man who came to Jesus always kept?

I: What 'I' was used to make chariots?

F _ _ _ _ _ _ _ _   P _ _ _ _ _ _ _

K _ _ _ _ _ _ _ _   T _ _ _ _ _ _ _

U _ _ _ _ _ _ _ _   S _ _ _ _ _ _ _

V _ _ _ _ _ _ _ _   B _ _ _ _ _ _ _

A _ _ _ _ _ _ _ _   N _ _ _ _ _ _ _

E _ _ _ _ _ _ _ _   M _ _ _ _ _ _ _

C _ _ _ _ _ _ _ _   H _ _ _ _ _ _ _

R _ _ _ _ _ _ _ _   O _ _ _ _ _ _ _

I _ _ _ _ _ _ _ _   D _ _ _ _ _ _ _

G _ _ _ _ _ _ _ _   L _ _ _ _ _ _ _

40

F: What 'F' should be laid on rock?

K: What 'K' in the Desert of Zin was where Moses struck a rock to find water?

U: What 'U' mentioned by Zechariah is a day without light or night?

V: What 'V' is another word for slave?

A: What 'A' is an Aramaic word, often untranslated meaning 'Father'?

E: What 'E' was the son of Shaphat?

C: What 'C' is an English town famous for its twisted spire?

R: What 'R' did Peter see in his vision in Joppa?

I: What 'I' was the son of Hagar?

G: What 'G' were the people whom Joshua made wood-cutters and water-carriers?

P: What 'P' was Pilate's title?

T: What 'T' was a Bible measure for gold and silver?

S: What 'S' is a Hyde Park preacher who became a life peer?

B: What 'B' was a friend of Job?

N: What 'N' was the city Jonah was told to go to?

M: What 'M' was another name for John son of Mary?

H: What 'H' received a letter from Sennacherib and spread it before the Lord?

O: What 'O' is copper smelted from?

D: What 'D' was a maker of robes and other clothing in Joppa?

L: What 'L' was one of the Asian churches mentioned in the Revelation?

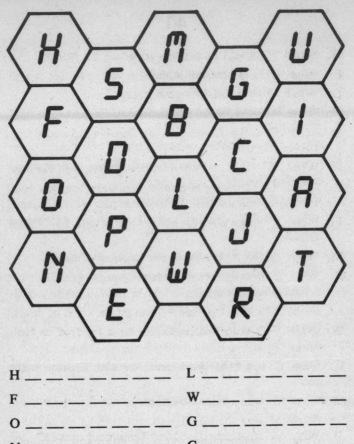

H _ _ _ _ _ _ _ _   L _ _ _ _ _ _ _

F _ _ _ _ _ _ _ _   W _ _ _ _ _ _ _

O _ _ _ _ _ _ _ _   G _ _ _ _ _ _ _

N _ _ _ _ _ _ _ _   C _ _ _ _ _ _ _ _

S _ _ _ _ _ _ _ _   J _ _ _ _ _ _ _

D _ _ _ _ _ _ _ _   R _ _ _ _ _ _ _

P _ _ _ _ _ _ _ _   U _ _ _ _ _ _ _

E _ _ _ _ _ _ _ _   I _ _ _ _ _ _ _

M _ _ _ _ _ _ _   A _ _ _ _ _ _ _

B _ _ _ _ _ _ _ _   T _ _ _ _ _ _ _

41

H: What 'H' was a king eaten to death by worms?

F: What 'F' is a pleasant smell?

O: What 'O' was David's grandfather?

N: What 'N' was father of Joshua?

S: What 'S' was besieged by King Ben-Hadad and thirty-two other kings?

D: What 'D' was a member of the Areopagus in Athens?

P: What 'P' besides grapes and figs were brought back from the Valley of Eshcol by the explorers in Canaan?

E: What 'E' was a Buzite who was angry with Job's three friends?

M: What 'M' in a parable is the smallest of seeds?

B: What 'B' was the town where the people examined the Scriptures every day?

L: What 'L' was a language written on the cross of Jesus?

W: What 'W' happened overnight to a fig tree in Holy Week?

G: What 'G' was the Bible name for the Mediterranean Sea?

C: What 'C' was a pillar which led the wandering Israelites by day?

J: What 'J' wrote the last New Testament epistle?

R: What 'R' split when Jesus died?

U: What 'U' is shouting all together or all singing the same part?

I: What 'I' prophesied the fall of Sennacherib?

A: What 'A' was the name Nebuchadnezzar gave to one of the Hebrew boys?

T: What 'T' was played by Miriam?

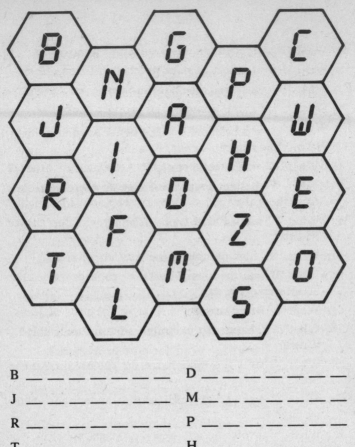

B _ _ _ _ _ _ _ _
J _ _ _ _ _ _ _ _
R _ _ _ _ _ _ _ _
T _ _ _ _ _ _ _ _
N _ _ _ _ _ _ _ _
I _ _ _ _ _ _ _ _
F _ _ _ _ _ _ _ _
L _ _ _ _ _ _ _ _
G _ _ _ _ _ _ _ _
A _ _ _ _ _ _ _ _

D _ _ _ _ _ _ _ _
M _ _ _ _ _ _ _ _
P _ _ _ _ _ _ _ _
H _ _ _ _ _ _ _ _
Z _ _ _ _ _ _ _ _
S _ _ _ _ _ _ _ _
C _ _ _ _ _ _ _ _
W _ _ _ _ _ _ _ _
E _ _ _ _ _ _ _ _
O _ _ _ _ _ _ _ _

42

B: What 'B' attended Sergius Paulus in Paphos?

J: What 'J' had a fleet of ships wrecked at Ezion Geber?

R: What 'R' was saved when Joshua destroyed Jericho?

T: What 'T' was the home of the prophet Amos?

N: What 'N' had a vineyard near Ahab's palace?

I: What 'I' was Jacob's changed name?

F: What 'F' is made by a plough?

L: What 'L' of Cyrene was a member of the church in Antioch?

G: What 'G' follows 'Tell it not in . . .'?

A: What 'A' stole gold and silver and a Babylonian robe during the Israelites' attack on Ai?

D: What 'D' was the wife of Felix?

M: What 'M' was the place where the Israelites could not drink the bitter water?

P: What 'P' was one of the figureheads on Paul's ship?

H: What 'H' is another word for port or harbour?

Z: What 'Z' was a city in the extreme south of Judah?

S: What 'S' was an Horonite who opposed Nehemiah's rebuilding plan for Jerusalem?

C: What 'C' did the soldiers cast lots for as they crucified Jesus?

W: What 'W' did the boy Jesus grow in besides stature?

E: What 'E' in Aramaic spoken by Jesus means 'be opened'?

O: What 'O' is an Irish society raised to defend the Protestant faith?

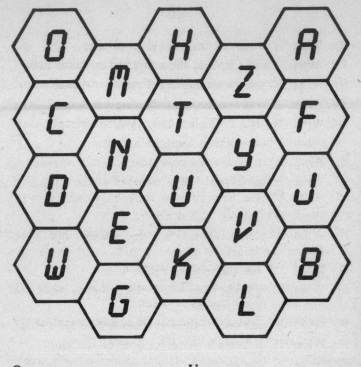

O _ _ _ _ _ _ _ _ _ _   U _ _ _ _ _ _ _

C _ _ _ _ _ _ _ _ _ _   K _ _ _ _ _ _ _

D _ _ _ _ _ _ _ _ _ _   Z _ _ _ _ _ _ _

W _ _ _ _ _ _ _ _ _ _   Y _ _ _ _ _ _ _

M _ _ _ _ _ _ _ _ _ _   V _ _ _ _ _ _ _

N _ _ _ _ _ _ _ _ _ _   L _ _ _ _ _ _ _

E _ _ _ _ _ _ _ _ _ _   A _ _ _ _ _ _ _

G _ _ _ _ _ _ _ _ _ _   F _ _ _ _ _ _ _

H _ _ _ _ _ _ _ _ _ _   J _ _ _ _ _ _ _

T _ _ _ _ _ _ _ _ _ _   B _ _ _ _ _ _ _

43

O: What 'O' was Naomi's daughter-in-law?

C: What 'C' was torn in the temple when Jesus died?

D: What 'D' was a woman Paul met in Athens?

W: What 'W' chewed the vine sheltering Jonah in Nineveh?

M: What 'M' was the field where Abraham buried Sarah?

N: What 'N' is another name for Christmas?

E: What 'E' was a well-versed teacher who returned to Jerusalem in the time of Artaxerxes?

G: What 'G' did the explorers bring to Moses from the Valley of Eshcol?

H: What 'H' was a priest who found the lost Book of the Law in Josiah's reign?

T: What 'T' was Abraham's father?

U: What 'U' was the bread the Israelites were to use during the feast in the month of Ahib?

K: What 'K' was a bird detestable to the Israelites?

Z: What 'Z' was a Jericho tax-collector?

Y: What 'Y' was Rebekah told the older would serve?

V: What 'V' was a queen of Persia?

L: What 'L' was a city where Paul was stoned and thought to be dead?

A: What 'A' was the special annual day for the Israelites to pray for forgiveness for their sins?

F: What 'F' means powerless and useless?

J: What 'J' was a great soldier in David's time?

B: What 'B' is the vicinity in which the resurrected Jesus was taken up into heaven?

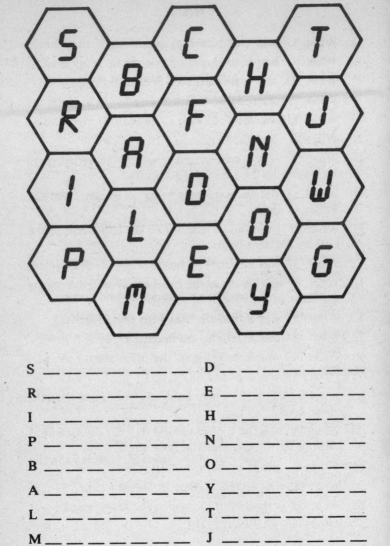

S _ _ _ _ _ _ _ _   D _ _ _ _ _ _ _ _
R _ _ _ _ _ _ _ _   E _ _ _ _ _ _ _ _
I _ _ _ _ _ _ _ _   H _ _ _ _ _ _ _ _
P _ _ _ _ _ _ _ _   N _ _ _ _ _ _ _ _
B _ _ _ _ _ _ _ _   O _ _ _ _ _ _ _ _
A _ _ _ _ _ _ _ _   Y _ _ _ _ _ _ _ _
L _ _ _ _ _ _ _ _   T _ _ _ _ _ _ _ _
M _ _ _ _ _ _ _ _   J _ _ _ _ _ _ _ _
C _ _ _ _ _ _ _ _   W _ _ _ _ _ _ _ _
F _ _ _ _ _ _ _ _   G _ _ _ _ _ _ _ _

44

S: What 'S' did the Ninevites wear when they heard Jonah's message?

R: What 'R' were the cities set aside by Joshua where unintentional killers could flee for safety?

I: What 'I' was son of Jacob and Leah?

P: What 'P' were the people with whom Samson asked to die?

B: What 'B' married a Moabitess and became the great-grandfather of King David?

A: What 'A' is a Bible name for the Dead Sea?

L: What 'L' was another name for Matthew?

M: What 'M' was a Jew in Susa who adopted Esther?

C: What 'C' was made of gold and wrongly worshipped by the Israelites?

F: What 'F' was Jesus to tax-collectors and sinners?

D: What 'D' comes before way, post and keeper?

E: What 'E' was a son of Isaac and became a mighty hunter?

H: What 'H' was a prophetess in Jerusalem in Josiah's reign?

N: What 'N' did Artaxerxes send to Jerusalem to rebuild it?

O: What 'O' was a deliverer of the Israelites in the days of the judges?

Y: What 'Y' was a colour of the riders' breastplates in the Relevation?

T: What 'T' pairs with Urim?

J: What 'J' received the order from   r-old Moses to be strong and courageous?

W: What 'W' put more into the temple treasury than anyone else?

G: What 'G' was the angel who appeared to Mary?

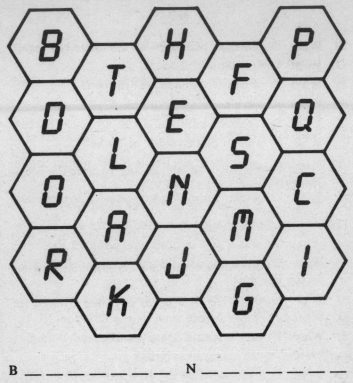

B _ _ _ _ _ _ _ _   N _ _ _ _ _ _ _
D _ _ _ _ _ _ _   J _ _ _ _ _ _ _
O _ _ _ _ _ _ _   F _ _ _ _ _ _ _
R _ _ _ _ _ _ _   S _ _ _ _ _ _ _
T _ _ _ _ _ _ _   M _ _ _ _ _ _ _
L _ _ _ _ _ _ _   G _ _ _ _ _ _ _
A _ _ _ _ _ _ _   P _ _ _ _ _ _ _
K _ _ _ _ _ _ _   Q _ _ _ _ _ _ _
H _ _ _ _ _ _ _   C _ _ _ _ _ _ _
E _ _ _ _ _ _ _   I _ _ _ _ _ _ _

45

B: What 'B' did Esau sell to Jacob for some red stew?

D: What 'D' is a mournful song?

O: What 'O' was where Jonah was thrown?

R: What 'R' were crucified with Jesus?

T: What 'T' was the home of Lydia, the purple-cloth seller?

L: What 'L' was an earlier name of Bethel?

A: What 'A' fell through the lattice of his upper room in Samaria?

K: What 'K' besides cups and pitchers were ceremonially washed by Jews?

H: What 'H' tried to destroy the Jews in Queen Esther's day?

E: What 'E' was the place where the Israelites found twelve springs?

N: What 'N' was a German pastor who was arrested for his faith?

J: What 'J' was Naboth's home town?

F: What 'F' sets a snare for birds?

S: What 'S' is the name of the Hebrews' day of rest?

M: What 'M' was the wandering Israelites' food which tasted like honey wafers?

G: What 'G' was a son of Jacob meaning good fortune?

P: What 'P' was the chief official of Malta?

Q: What 'Q' did Paul fear was among the Corinthians?

C: What 'C' means a gift devoted to God?

I: What 'I' was the country Aquila and Priscilla lived in before they settled in Corinth?

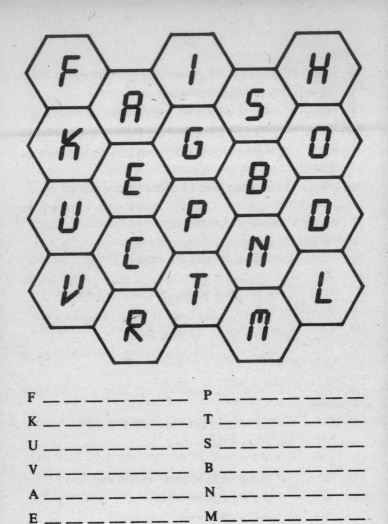

F _ _ _ _ _ _ _ _   P _ _ _ _ _ _

K _ _ _ _ _ _ _ _   T _ _ _ _ _ _

U _ _ _ _ _ _ _ _   S _ _ _ _ _ _

V _ _ _ _ _ _ _ _   B _ _ _ _ _ _

A _ _ _ _ _ _ _ _   N _ _ _ _ _ _

E _ _ _ _ _ _ _ _   M _ _ _ _ _ _

C _ _ _ _ _ _ _ _   H _ _ _ _ _ _

R _ _ _ _ _ _ _ _   O _ _ _ _ _ _

I _ _ _ _ _ _ _ _   D _ _ _ _ _ _

G _ _ _ _ _ _ _ _   L _ _ _ _ _ _

46

F: What 'F' lasted seven years in Egypt in Joseph's time?

K: What 'K' was a son of Naomi?

U: What 'U' was a source of gold known to Jeremiah?

V: What 'V' was seen hanging from Paul's hand in Malta?

A: What 'A' was an elderly prophetess delighted to see the baby Jesus?

E: What 'E' was the first of Job's three-friends?

C: What 'C' was the King of Persia who restored the temple vessels to Jerusalem?

R: What 'R' are gems of less value than wisdom?

I: What 'I' is to call on God in prayer?

G: What 'G' was the camp where Joshua set up twelve stones after crossing Jordan?

P: What 'P' did everyone hold John the Baptist to be?

T: What 'T' often links up with Sidon?

S: What 'S' was the mountain where God gave his law to Moses?

B: What 'B' was the country of King Jehoiachin's captivity?

N: What 'N' is the central aisle of a church?

M: What 'M' means: 'May the Lord keep watch between you and me'?

H: What 'H' comes before long, waters and way?

O: What 'O' is a screeching bird?

D: What 'D' was a daughter of Jacob?

L: What 'L' was Jacob's first wife?

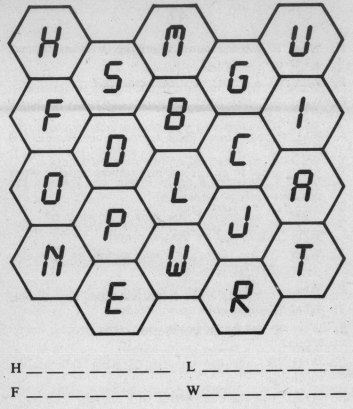

H _ _ _ _ _ _ _ _   L _ _ _ _ _ _ _ _

F _ _ _ _ _ _ _ _   W _ _ _ _ _ _ _ _

O _ _ _ _ _ _ _ _   G _ _ _ _ _ _ _ _

N _ _ _ _ _ _ _ _   C _ _ _ _ _ _ _ _

S _ _ _ _ _ _ _ _   J _ _ _ _ _ _ _ _

D _ _ _ _ _ _ _ _   R _ _ _ _ _ _ _ _

P _ _ _ _ _ _ _ _   U _ _ _ _ _ _ _ _

E _ _ _ _ _ _ _ _   I _ _ _ _ _ _ _ _

M _ _ _ _ _ _ _ _   A _ _ _ _ _ _ _ _

B _ _ _ _ _ _ _ _   T _ _ _ _ _ _ _ _

47

H: What 'H' was the mount where the Israelites stripped off their ornaments?

F: What 'F' is a river or stream crossing?

O: What 'O' was used to strike down six hundred Philistines?

N: What 'N' was Simon Peter washing when Jesus called him?

S: What 'S' did Joseph accuse his brothers of being when they visited him in Egypt?

D: What 'D' is a royal crown?

P: What 'P' is a festival to commemorate the Jews' deliverance in Persia?

E: What 'E' was the main garment for the priests in the time of Moses?

M: What 'M' was the name Nebuchadnezzar gave to one of the Hebrew boys?

B: What 'B' did Elijah sacrifice on Carmel?

L: What 'L' is a flower of the valley?

W: What 'W' blew Elijah up to heaven?

G: What 'G' was Jesus thought to be when walking on the water?

C: What 'C' must be taken up when we follow Jesus?

J: What 'J' received from his father a richly ornamented robe?

R: What 'R' were used to drop Jeremiah into a cistern?

U: What 'U' means righteous and honest?

I: What 'I' was on Caesar's coins?

A: What 'A' was the wood used to make the ark for the Israelites?

T: What 'T' does the Lord prepare before me in the presence of my enemies?

B _ _ _ _ _ _ _

J _ _ _ _ _ _ _

R _ _ _ _ _ _ _

T _ _ _ _ _ _ _

N _ _ _ _ _ _ _

I _ _ _ _ _ _ _

F _ _ _ _ _ _ _

L _ _ _ _ _ _ _

G _ _ _ _ _ _ _

A _ _ _ _ _ _ _

D _ _ _ _ _ _ _

M _ _ _ _ _ _ _

P _ _ _ _ _ _ _

H _ _ _ _ _ _ _

Z _ _ _ _ _ _ _

S _ _ _ _ _ _ _

C _ _ _ _ _ _ _

W _ _ _ _ _ _ _

E _ _ _ _ _ _ _

O _ _ _ _ _ _ _

48

B: What 'B' was filled with the Spirit of God to become a metal-worker?

J: What 'J' was a blameless man who lived in Uz?

R: What 'R' was a two-horned animal in Daniel's vision?

T: What 'T' is remembered as the doubting apostle?

N: What 'N' was the role of the mother of Moses to her baby?

I: What 'I' is the smallest Greek letter?

F: What 'F' was the type of chariot in which Elijah went to heaven?

L: What 'L' is a ten-stringed musical instrument?

G: What 'G' is to die if to live is Christ?

A: What 'A' did Jeshua and Zerubbabel first rebuild in Jeusalem in the days of Cyrus?

D: What 'D' was the part of Easter Day when the women found an empty tomb?

M: What 'M' was more humble than anyone else on the face of the earth?

P: What 'P' was an Egyptian captain of the guard who bought Joseph as a slave?

H: What 'H' with Aaron held up the hands of Moses before the Amalekites?

Z: What 'Z' was an Old Testament prophet, son of Cushi?

S: What 'S' was near the place where Joseph's brothers grazed their father's flocks?

C: What 'C' did both Elijah and Elisha use to strike the Jordan?

W: What 'W' did a man in a parable build in his vineyard?

E: What 'E' is another name for a king's ambassador?

O: What 'O' was a bad one at the tomb of Lazarus?

Solution: Puzzle 1

O: Over; C: Carmel; D: Dead; W: Weatherhead;
M: Mesopotamia; N: Naboth; E: Esther; G: Grace;
H: Heathen; T: Treasures; U: Under; K: King; Z: Zeus;
Y: Yield; V: Victory; L: Leviathan; A: Ananias; F: For;
J: Jarrow; B: Bells.

Solution: Puzzle 2

S: Sanhedrin; R: Rachel; I: Idol; P: Pilate; B: Babel;
A: Adam; L: Levites; M: Moses; C: Candace; F: Figs;
D: Daniel; E: Eli; H: Happy; N: Nicopolis; O: Over;
Y: Yield; T: Tomer; J: John; W: Wesley; G: Gallio.

Solution: Puzzle 3

B: Bishop; D: Devil; O: Oxford; R: Rephidim;
T: Tiberius; L: Luke; A: Archbishop; K: Knox;
H: Holy; E: Egypt; N: Naaman; J: Jerusalem; F: Finger;
S: Selah; M: Malta; G: Gate; P: Paphos; Q: Quail;
C: Caleb; I: Ignatius.

Solution: Puzzle 4

F: Festus; K: King; U: Uncle; V: Vatican; A: Arimathea;
E: Ehud; C: Cephas; R: Rochester; I: Ichabod;
G: Graham; P: Philip; T: Taxes; S: Salome; B: Beth;
N: Nazareth; M: Mark; H: Howe; O: Oberammergau;
D: Delta; L: Livingstone.

Solution: Puzzle 5

H: Hazael; F: Fiji; O: Ophir; N: Noah; S: Saul; D: Demas;
P: Philemon; E: Ethiopia; M: Malachi; B: Bethlehem;
L: Lambeth; W: White; G: Gamaliel; C: Columba; J: Jordan;
R: Revelation; U: Uriah; I: Italy; A: Amos; T: Truro.

Solution: Puzzle 6

B: Barnabas; J: Jeremiah; R: Ruth; T: Third; N: Nile;
I: Iona; F: Frogs; L: Luther; G: Greek; A: Apostles;
D: Dante; M: Messiah; P: Parchment; H: Hannah;
Z: Zebedee; S: Samson; C: Calabar; W: Whitechapel;
E: Elijah; O: Obadiah.

Solution: Puzzle 7

O: Og; C: Cain; D: David; W: Walls; M: Mediterranean;
N: New; E: Evil; G: Galilee; H: Heaven; T: Timothy;
U: Uzziah; K: Kidron; Z: Zoo; Y: York; V: Vulgate;
L: Love; A: Andrew; F: Fish; J: John; B: Booth.

Solution: Puzzle 8

S: Schweitzer; R: Ramsey; I: Iran; P: Purple; B: Bethany;
A: Ascension; L: Liverpool; M: Moab; C: Cain; F: Felix;
D: Donald; E: Easter; H: Hankey; N: Norman; O: On;
Y: Youth; T: Tiber; J: John; W: Westminster; G: Ganges.

Solution: Puzzle 9

B: Benjamin; D: Down; O: Omer; R: Rehoboam; T: Temple;
L: Light; A: Aaron; K: Kine; H: Ham; E: Eden; N: Nun;
J: Joel; F: Friendship; S: Solomon; M: Moody; G: Gideon;
P: Psalms; Q: Quirinius; C: Cana; I: Isaac.

Solution: Puzzle 10

F: Faith; K: Knock; U: Up; V: Valletta; A: Areopagus;
E: Eli; C: Congregational; R: Rib; I: Incarnation; G: Gerizim;
P: Priscilla; T: Tishbite; S: Sheppard; B: Belshazzar;
N: Nahor; M: Magi; H: Hyssop; O: Ophrah; D: Demetrius;
L: Lord's.

Solution: Puzzle 11

H: Head; F: Fifth; O: Offering; N: Needle; S: Studd;
D: Decapolis; P: Priest; E: Elkanah; M: Moderator;
B: Beersheba; L: Love; W: Water; G: Gold; C: Colosseum;
J: John; R: Rufus; U: Unclean; I: Immanuel; A: Ararat;
T: Tongue.

Solution: Puzzle 12

B: Beelzebub; J: Jubal; R: Ruth; T: Theophilus; N: Nahum;
I: Iscariot; F: First; L: Lazarus; G: Gentiles; A: Alphaeus;
D: David; M: Methuselah; P: Phylacteries; H: Hellenists;
Z: Zipporah; S: Storm; C: Captain; W: Wilderness; E: Eagle;
O: Olives.

Solution: Puzzle 13

O: Obey;   C: Calvary;   D: Deborah;   W: Weeds;   M: Midianites;
N: Nebuchadnezzar;   E: Elijah;   G: Green;   H: Herod;
T: Testament;   U: Usury;   K: King;   Z: Zedekiah   Y: Yoke;
V: Vicar;   L: Lions;   A: Ananias;   F: Fulfil;   J: Jethro;
B: Baker.

Solution: Puzzle 14

S: Sychar;   R: Razor;   I: Inn;   P: Prince;   B: Barnardo;
A: Apochrypha;   L: Lion;   M: Mark;   C: Capernaum;   F: Feast;
D: Dream;   E: Elizabeth;   H: Hypocrite;   N: Nile;   O: Onesimus;
Y: Yoke;   T: Troas;   J: Jephthah;   W: Waltham;   G: Good.

Solution: Puzzle 15

B: Bush;   D: Date;   O: Off;   R: Riddle;   T: Tarshish;   L: Laban;
A: Aylward;   K: Kish;   H: Holes;   E: Erastus;   N: Narrow;
J: Judea;   F: Foolish;   S: Salisbury;   M: Manassah;   G: Goliath;
P: Plumb-line;   Q: Quarry;   C: Centurion;   I: Italian.

Solution: Puzzle 16

F: Fire;   K: Kenite;   U: Uzza;   V: Valley;   A: Abner;
E: Egyptian;   C: Cup;   R: Rejoice;   I: Iniquity;   G: General;
P: Pearl;   T: Trophimus;   S: Serpent;   B: Babylon;   N: Nympha;
M: Manoah;   H: Honey;   O: Onyx;   D: Destruction;   L: Lent.

Solution: Puzzle 17

H: Hermes;   F: Flax;   O: Out;   N: Nimrod;   S: Shamgar;
D: Dura;   P: Pigs;   E: Ebenezer;   M: Michal;   B: Beatitudes;
L: Lois;   W: Washington;   G: Goshen;   C: Christening;
J: Jehovah;   R: Rabboni;   U: Under;   I: India;   A: Agag;
T: Tertullus.

Solution: Puzzle 18

B: Becket;   J: Jabbok;   R: Refiner;   T: Tetrarch;   N: Nicolaitans;
I: Ira;   F: Fox;   L: Light;   G: Grenfell;   A: Adullam;
D: Diotrephas;   M: Matthew;   P: Paul;   H: Hosanna;
Z: Zion;   S: Shiloh;   C: Cornfields;   W: William;   E: Endor;
O: Onions.

Solution: Puzzle 19

O: Onesiphorus; C: Canterbury; D: David; W: Wesley;
M: Mene; N: Nod; E: Ezekiel; G: Good; H: Hermogenes;
T: Tomorrow; U: Urim; K: Keep; Z: Zechariah Y: Yeast;
V: Vine; L: Lamentations; A: Advent; F: Farmer; J: Joses;
B: Belteshazzar.

Solution: Puzzle 20

S: Snake; R: Raven; I: Ivory; P: Pisa; B: Bethany;
A: Agabus; L: Lady; M: Maundy; C: Cleopas; F: Furnace;
D: Donkey; E: Edict; H: Hail; N: Nard; O: Oracle;
Y: Yarn; T: Timothy; J: Joppa; W: With; G: Gilboa.

Solution: Puzzle 21

B: Beautiful; D: Dove; O: Ox; R: Rhodes; T: Tamarisk;
L: Locusts; A: Archelaus; K: Korazin; H: Hophni; E: Exalted;
N: Nimshi; J: Job; F: Forgiveness; S: Sisera; M: Malchus;
G: Gomer; P: Place; Q: Quarters; C: Curate; I: Isaiah.

Solution: Puzzle 22

F: Francis; K: Kios; U: Unknown; V: Vestments; A: Absalom;
E: Eucharist; C: Canticles; R: Reaper; I: Ichabod;
G: Gennesaret; P: Pope; T: Thief; S: Scroll; B: Bridegroom;
N: Nathaniel; M: Matthias; H: Helena; O: Obadiah; D: Dove;
L: Life.

Solution: Puzzle 23

H: Holy; F: Fasting; O: Omega; N: News; S: Stanley;
D: Debts; P: Patriarch; E: Ebenezer; M: Macedonia;
B: Baruch; L: Last; W: Wilberforce; G: Goats; C: Camel;
J: Jonathan; R: Reuben; U: Usher; I: Ish-Boseth;
A: Authority; T: Tigris.

Solution: Puzzle 24

B: Bathsheba; J: Jairus; R: Ransom; T: Tyndale; N: Name;
I: Immortal; F: Fruit; L: Leather; G: Good; A: Araunah;
D: Dagon; M: Mnason; P: Pilate; H: Hebron; Z: Zena;
S: Seth; C: Cliff; W: Way; E: Elymas; O: Origen.

Solution: Puzzle 25

O: Oswald; C: Compassion; D: Down; W: Whispering;
M: Mephibosheth; N: Noon; E: Elstow; G: Grey; H: Hunt;
T: Taxes; U: Up; K: Kebar; Z: Zadok; Y: Yesterday;
V: Voice; L: Legion; A: Adonijah; F: Feet; J: Jonathan;
B: Barnabas.

Solution: Puzzle 26

S: Simon; R: Ramah; I: Isaac; P: Pool; B: Bones;
A: Arabs; L: Leopard; M: Money; C: Cymbal; F: Fever;
D: Discerning; E: Eutychus; H: Hand; N: Numbers;
O: Orphans; Y: Yeast; T: Tabernacle; J: James; W: Word;
G: Gaius.

Solution: Puzzle 27

B: Benediction; D: Desert; O: Organ; R: Rainbow;
T: Timothy; L: Locusts; A: Azotus; K: Kiss; H: Hades;
E: Ephesians; N: Niger; J: Jason; F: Fishermen; S: Straw;
M: Magdalene; G: Grasshoppers; P: Persecution; Q: Quartus;
C: Cock; I: Invisible.

Solution: Puzzle 28

F: Font; K: Kindness; U: Unbeliever; V: Vigil; A: Athens;
E: Evangelist; C: Conclave; R: Roman; I: Innocent;
G: Gregory; P: Philippi; T: Tombs; S: Seven; B: Bithynia;
N: Never; M: Manaen; H: Harvest; O: Ocean; D: Damascus;
L: Lot.

Solution: Puzzle 29

H: Hell; F: Feathers; O: Oratorio; N: Name; S: Siddim;
D: Doors; P: Perga; E: Euodia; M: Mediator; B: Blood;
L: Lebanon; W: Worship; G: Gladstone; C: Chosen;
J: Jeremiah; R: Right; U: Un; I: Ink; A: Amoz; T: Thunder.

Solution: Puzzle 30

B: Bears; J: Joseph; R: Rich; T: Tekel; N: Neighbour;
I: Images; F: Firstfruits; L: Leper; G: Galilee; A: Ash;
D: Day; M: Martha; P: Potter; H: Hagar; Z: Zin;
S: Salt; C: Christians; W: Whitsun; E: Emerald; O: Orion.

Solution: Puzzle 31

O: Oars; C: Claudius; D: Debts; W: Wadi; M: Mamre;
N: Nabal; E: Ecclesiastes; G: Gold; H: Horse;
T: Tiberias; U: Useful; K: Kerith; Z: Zither; Y: Young;
V: Venom; L: Last; A: Agabus; F: Field; J: Judas;
B: Babbler.

Solution: Puzzle 32

S: Sheba; R: Recabites; I: Ibex; P: Plain; B: Barabbas;
A: Alabaster; L: Lollards; M: Manger; C: Cyrene; F: Flute;
D: Didymus; E: Emmaus; H: Hallelujah; N: Nail; O: Oak;
Y: Yelling; T: Thirty; J: Jubilee; W: Wages; G: Gethsemane.

Solution: Puzzle 33

B: Balm; D: David; O: Off; R: Red; T: Thorns; L: Lamb;
A: Alpha; K: Keys; H: Haggai; E: Elimelech; N: Nain;
J: Japheth; F: Flogging; S: Shunem; M: Mitre; G: Gomorrah;
P: Pisgah; Q: Queen; C: Counsellor; I: Ice.

Solution: Puzzle 34

F: Fox; K: Kind; U: Ur; V: Visions; A: Abel; E: Epicureans;
C: Child; R: Rabbi; I: Incense; G: Gehazi; P: Parables;
T: True; S: Shishak; B: Boanerges; N: Nomads; M: Melon;
H: Handsome; O: Olives; D: Denarius; L: Locusts.

Solution: Puzzle 35

H: Haran; F: Flour; O: Ordination; N: Naomi; S: Shadrach;
D: Desert; P: Passover; E: Earthquake; M: Medes; B: Bread;
L: Lazarus; W: Wailing; G: George; C: Crispus; J: Jasper;
R: Ravens; U: Uz; I: Inheritance; A: Abraham; T: Tarsus.

Solution: Puzzle 36

B: Baal; J: Jericho; R: Robe; T: Tertius; N: Narcissus;
I: Iconium; F: Fire; L: Lamp; G: Golgotha; A: Annas;
D: Decapolis; M: Micah; P: Puteoli; H: Harp; Z: Zarephath;
S: Stones; C: Caesar; W: Wreaths; E: Epenetus;
O: Ordinances.

Solution: Puzzle 37

O: Obstacle; C: Cloud; D: Dis; W: Waves; M: Moriah;
N: Nathan; E: Ephraim; G: Galatians; H: Hundred;
T: Tombs; U: Unit; K: Kings; Z: Zoar; Y: Year's;
V: Vow; L: Lydda; A: Accent; F: Foal; J: Jesse;
B: Boston.

Solution: Puzzle 38

S: Synagogues; R: Rhoda; I: Instructor; P: Proverbs;
B: Bartimaeus; A: Andrew; L: Leprosy; M: Melchizedek;
C: Coin; F: Foe; D: Doctrine; E: Earth; H: Hazael;
N: Nebo; O: Omri; Y: Youth; T: Tabitha; J: Jonah;
W: Wax; G: Gaza.

Solution: Puzzle 39

B: Balaam; D: Derbe; O: Observe; R: Rock; T: Thessalonica;
L: Language; A: Aijalon; K: Kishon; H: Hoshea; E: Epistles;
N: Nests; J: Josiah; F: Foot; S: Salt; M: Moth;
G: Guildford; P: Phoenix; Q: Questions; C: Commandments;
I: Iron.

Solution: Puzzle 40

F: Foundation; K: Kadesh; U: Unique; V: Vassal; A: Abba;
E: Elisha; C: Chesterfield; R: Reptiles; I: Ishmael;
G: Gibeonites; P: Pontius; T: Talent; S: Soper; B: Bildad;
N: Nineveh; M: Mark; H: Hezekiah; O: Ore; D: Dorcas;
L: Laodicea.

Solution: Puzzle 41

H: Herod; F: Fragrance; O: Obed; N: Nun; S: Samaria;
D: Dionysius; P: Pomegranates; E: Elihu; M: Mustard;
B: Berea; L: Latin; W: Withered; G: Great; C: Cloud;
J: Jude; R: Rocks; U: Unison; I: Isaiah; A: Abednego;
T: Tambourine.

Solution: Puzzle 42

B: Bar-Jesus; J: Jehoshaphat; R: Rahab; T: Tekoa;
N: Naboth; I: Israel; F: Furrow; L: Lucius; G: Gath;
A: Achan; D: Druscilla; M: Marah; P: Pollux; H: Haven;
Z: Ziklag; S: Sanballat; C: Clothes; W: Wisdom;
E: Ephphatha; O: Orange.

Solution: Puzzle 43

O: Orpah; C: Curtain; D: Damascus; W: Worm;
M: Machpelah; N: Noel; E: Ezra; G: Grapes; H: Hilkiah;
T: Terah; U: Unleavened; K: Kite; Z: Zacchaeus; Y: Younger;
V: Vashti; L: Lystra; A: Atonement; F: Futile; J: Joab;
B: Bethany.

Solution: Puzzle 44

S: Sackcloth; R: Refuge; I: Issachar; P: Philistines;
B: Boaz; A: Arabah; L: Levi; M: Mordecai; C: Calf;
F: Friend; D: Door; E: Esau; H: Huldah; N: Nehemiah;
O: Othniel; Y: Yellow; T: Thummim; J: Joshua; W: Widow;
G: Gabriel.

Solution: Puzzle 45

B: Birthright; D: Dirge; O: Overboard; R: Robbers;
T: Thyatira; L: Luz; A: Ahaziah; K: Kettles; H: Haman;
E: Elim; N: Niemöller; J: Jezreel; F: Fowler; S: Sabbath;
M: Manna; G: Gad; P: Publius; Q: Quarrelling; C: Corban;
I: Italy.

Solution: Puzzle 46

F: Famine; K: Kilion; U: Uphaz; V: Viper; A: Anna;
E: Eliphaz; C: Cyrus; R: Rubies; I: Invoke; G: Gilgal;
P: Prophet; T: Tyre; S: Sinai; B: Babylon; N: Nave;
M: Mizpah; H: Head; O: Owl; D: Dinah; L: Leah.

Solution: Puzzle 47

H: Horeb; F: Ford; O: Oxgoad; N: Nets; S: Spies;
D: Diadem; P: Purim; E: Ephod; M: Meshach; B: Bull;
L: Lily; W: Whirlwind; G: Ghost; C: Cross; J: Joseph;
R: Ropes; U: Upright; I: Inscription; A: Acacia; T: Table.

Solution: Puzzle 48

B: Bezalel; J: Job; R: Ram; T: Thomas; N: Nurse; I: Iota;
F: Fire; L: Lyre; G: Gain; A: Altar; D: Dawn; M: Moses;
P: Potiphar; H: Hur; Z: Zephaniah; S: Shechem; C: Cloak;
W: Watchtower; E: Envoy; O: Odour.